A Tax Guide to Pay and Perks

Contents

Preface to the Revised Edition   xiii

1. PERSONAL TAXATION IN GENERAL   1
   1.1   Introduction   1
   1.2   The Schedules   2
   1.3   Scope of Schedule E   2
   1.4   An 'office or employment'   3
   1.5   Schedule D or Schedule E   3
   1.6   Husband and wife   5
   1.7   Treatment of the wife's earned income   6

2. EMOLUMENTS   10
   2.1   Definition – what is included   10
   2.2   Payments which cannot be taxed at source   11
   2.3   Concessions   12
       2.3.1 Luncheon vouchers   12
       2.3.2 Long-service awards   12
       2.3.3 Removal expenses   13

3. ASSESSING AND COLLECTING THE TAX   15
   3.1   Introduction   15

Contents

3.2	PAYE	16
3.3	Coding	17
3.4	Deduction working sheets	18
3.5	Assessments: underpayments and overpayments	18
3.6	Basis of assessment	20
	3.6.1 Earnings basis	21
	3.6.2 Accounts year basis	23
	3.6.3 Timing of PAYE and national insurance payments	25
3.7	Unpaid emoluments	27
3.8	Concessional repayments	27
3.9	National insurance contributions	28
3.10	PAYE audit	30
4. EXPENSES		**32**
4.1	Allowable deductions	32
4.2	'Wholly and exclusively'	32
4.3	'Necessarily'	33
4.4	'In the performance of . . .'	34
4.5	Expenses specifically allowed by statute	35
4.6	Flat-rate expenses	35
4.7	Business entertaining expenses	36
4.8	Travelling expenses	37
4.9	Subscriptions	38
4.10	Round-sum allowances	39
4.11	Other expenses – general notes	39
5. FRINGE BENEFITS – BASIC RULES		**41**
5.1	Introduction	41
5.2	Salary or benefit?	42

Contents

5.3	Who falls to be taxed?	44
5.4	The £8500 threshold	44
5.5	Valuing benefits – directors and higher-paid employees	45
5.6	Valuing benefits – employees earning less than £8500	47
5.7	Returns and dispensations	49

6. FRINGE BENEFITS – SPECIFIC LEGISLATION — 50
6.1	Taxable benefits–summary chart	50
6.2	Vouchers	52
6.3	Living accommodation	54
	6.3.1 Occupier for rating purposes	57
	6.3.2 Representative occupation for director/higher-paid employees	58
6.4	Directors' PAYE	60

7. THE COMPANY CAR — 61
7.1	Introduction	61
7.2	'Table' benefits	62
7.3	'Pool' cars	64
7.4	Petrol	64
7.5	Collecting the tax	66
7.6	Employee-owned cars	67

8. BENEFICIAL LOAN ARRANGEMENTS — 69
8.1	Introduction	69
8.2	Effect of the legislation	69
8.3	Exemptions	70
8.4	Computing the chargeable benefit	72
8.5	Loan waivers	73

Contents

9. ACQUISITION OF SHARES BY
   EMPLOYEES   74
   9.1   Introduction   74
   9.2   Approved share options – the
          1984 scheme   74
          9.2.1 Participants and their
                participation   75
          9.2.2 Scheme shares   76
          9.2.3 Grant, exercise and transfer of
                options   77
   9.3   Unapproved share options   78
   9.4   Savings-related share-option
          schemes   81
   9.5   Anti-avoidance legislation and pitfalls   83
          9.5.1 Acquisitions at undervalue   83
          9.5.2 Non-exempted acquisitions   83
          9.5.3 'Stop-loss' arrangements   85
   9.6   Returns and information   85
   9.7   Profit-sharing schemes   86

10. PENSIONS FOR THE EMPLOYED   88
    10.1   The role of the State   88
    10.2   The State scheme   89
    10.3   Private schemes – requirements for
           approval   90
           10.3.1 Definition of 'final salary'   91
    10.4   Approval refused – the consequences   92
    10.5   Guaranteed minimum pensions   93
    10.6   Pension rights when changing jobs   94
    10.7   Termination of employment – con-
           tributions made   95

Contents

10.8	Self-administered pension schemes	95
10.9	Sick-pay and disability schemes	96
10.10	Death-in-service and accident policies	98
10.11	'Top-hat' and 'key-man' schemes	99
10.12	Additional voluntary contributions	100
10.13	Personal pension plans	101
	10.13.1 Capital commutation and transfer	103
	10.13.2 Loanback arrangements	104

11. TERMINATION PAYMENTS — 106
11.1	Introduction	106
11.2	Capital or income	107
11.3	Exempt lump sums	109
11.4	Tax-free part of a lump sum	110
11.5	The old and the new – which rules apply	110
11.6	The charge to tax	111
11.7	Redundancy payments	113
11.8	Restrictive covenants	113
11.9	Variation of service agreements	115
11.10	Inducing an employee to give up employment	116
11.11	The employer's position	116

12. BRITISH NATIONALS WORKING OVERSEAS — 119
12.1	Introduction	119
12.2	Domicile	119
12.3	Residence and ordinary residence	120
	12.3.1 Husband and wife	122

Contents

	12.3.2 Available accommodation	122
	12.3.3 Procedure	123
12.4	Employment earnings of non-residents	123
12.5	Personal allowances for non-residents	124
12.6	Double taxation relief	129
	12.6.1 The UK's double taxation agreements	130
12.7	Employment earnings of residents	132
12.8	The '100 per cent' deduction for long absences abroad	134
12.9	The '25 per cent' deduction for short absences abroad	137
12.10	Seamen and aircrew	139
12.11	Oil-rig workers	140
12.12	Travelling expenses	140
12.13	Unremittable overseas income	142
12.14	Collection of tax	143
12.15	National insurance contributions	144
12.16	Non-tax considerations	144

13.	FOREIGN NATIONALS WORKING IN THE UK	147
13.1	General rules	147
13.2	Income from UK resident employer	149
13.3	Income from employer not resident in the UK	149
13.4	Remittance basis	153
13.5	Collection of tax	155
13.6	Reimbursed expenses and fringe benefits	155
	13.6.1 Travelling expenses	156

13.7	Rent paid on UK property to non-resident landlord	157
13.8	Banking arrangements – general	158
	13.8.1 Banking arrangements – husband and wife	162
	13.8.2 Constructive remittances	163
13.9	National insurance contributions	165
13.10	Non-tax considerations	166
14.	TAX-PLANNING HINTS	167
14.1	Introduction	167
14.2	Pay the correct amount	167
14.3	Tax the correct amount	168
14.4	Lump-sum payments	169
14.5	Benefit from benefits	169
14.6	Beneficial loans	170
14.7	Educational assistance schemes	170
14.8	Remuneration or dividend?	172
14.9	A final word	175

APPENDIX A   176
Personal allowances 1984/85

APPENDIX B   177
Rates of income tax for 1984/85

APPENDIX C   178
National insurance contributions 1984/85

APPENDIX D   179
Benefits in kind – cars and car petrol 1984/85

Contents

APPENDIX E   181
    Income from which tax cannot be deducted at
    source
    Items not to be included in 'pay'

TABLES
    6.1   Taxable benefits   50
  12.1   UK tax liability on employment
            earnings – employer resident in UK,
            employee domiciled in UK   146

Preface to the Revised Edition

It is commonly assumed that there is very little that can be done to mitigate the tax position of individuals who are employed; tax and national insurance contributions are both deducted at source from the employee's regular pay packet under the apparently all-embracing PAYE system and there seems to be little scope for doing anything about it.

We believe that this is untrue and that is why we have written this book. First we look at how employment earnings and in particular fringe benefits are assessed to tax and how the tax is collected. We then look at other significant areas, such as acquisition of shares by employees, pensions, termination payments and the special position of individuals working overseas and of foreign nationals working in this country.

This is a book written for the layman, the taxpayer himself, rather than for the specialist, in the hope that he will understand a little more clearly how the system of taxation in this area works and how it affects him. For this reason we have not included references to the taxing Acts or to case law. In the final chapter we pull the threads together with some planning hints for the reader, which, with the advantage that an understanding of the system may give him, he can perhaps use to his benefit.

This revised edition is believed to reflect the law and practice of UK taxation in this area as it applied at 12 July 1984. In particular, it takes into account the significant changes in UK tax legislation introduced in the 1984 Finance Act, especially those relating to employee share option schemes (Chapter 9) and the tax treatment applicable to expatriates working overseas (Chapter 12) and those coming to work in this country (Chapter 13).

A final word of caution. The application of general ideas and concepts to any particular set of circumstances requires care and a full appreciation of the relevant facts. In looking at specific proposals or problems relating to his affairs, the reader should always seek professional advice. After the purchase of this book, this must be the next best investment that he can make.

1984

WRP
London
ESB
Leicester

1 Personal Taxation in General

1.1 Introduction

An individual's tax liability for any tax year (year ended 5 April) is computed as follows:

	£
Income	X
Less Deductions such as mortgage interest	(X)
Total statutory income	X
Personal allowances	(X)
Taxable income	£X

The personal allowances vary from year to year in accordance with the most recent Finance Act. A table showing personal allowances for the current year 1984/85 is included in Appendix A.

The tax liability is computed on a sliding scale in accordance with the tax rates for the year in question. For 1984/85 the rates vary from 30 per cent for taxable income up to

£15,400, to 60 per cent for taxable income exceeding £38,100. A table showing the tax rates for the current year can be found at Appendix B.

For years up to and including 1983/84 an additional tax (referred to as 'the investment income surcharge') was charged on the excess of investment income over a certain level (in 1983/84 this was fixed at £7,100). For 1984/85 and subsequent years this surcharge has been abolished, so that the distinction that previously applied between earned income and investment income has largely disappeared. The planning implications of this change are looked at in 14.8.

1.2 The Schedules

Each type of income is assessed under different 'Schedules' (A to F inclusive) and, within each Schedule, different sources of income may be assessed under different 'Cases'. All employment earnings are chargeable to tax under Schedule E.

1.3 Scope of Schedule E

Basically, the charge to tax arises in respect of the full amount of *emoluments* (see 2.1) in respect of an *office or employment* (defined below). Several types of benefit which are payable by the Department of Health and Social Security are also taxable as earned income, the most notable being national insurance retirement pensions, widows' benefits and unemployment benefits.

2

Payments under sick-pay and disability schemes are covered by special provisions – see 10.9.

Termination payments (whether contractual or ex-gratia) are taxable under Schedule E, subject to special provisions which are considered in Chapter 11.

1.4 An 'office or employment'

An *office* has been defined as a 'subsisting, permanent, substantive position which has an existence independent of the individual who filled it ...' such as a company director or chairman.

An *employment* is a formal relationship between a master and his servant and, to comply with UK employment legislation, the relationship must be evidenced by way of a legal contract of service. Such a 'contract of service' securing the relationship of master and servant must be distinguished from a 'contract for services' which is implicit in the carrying on of a trade, profession or vocation. In particular, if an individual derives income from more than one contract, his income from contracts of service will be taxable under Schedule E and that from contracts for services, under Schedule D.

1.5 Schedule D or Schedule E

There are distinct advantages in being taxed on earnings under Schedule D rather than Schedule E as regards method of payment of tax and the reliefs available in respect of expenses incurred. There are no comprehensive definitions or rules as to the distinction between earnings taxable under Schedule D or E (not even the definitions in 1.4 above). For example, although the position of an auditor has been judicially recognized as being an *office* the income therefrom is assessed under Schedule D.

It therefore becomes essentially a matter of *fact* and no one factor is conclusive. Based on the decisions in previous court cases, the Inland Revenue normally take the following factors as *favourable* in deciding if an individual should be assessed under Schedule D:

(1) the number of concurrent contracts held by the individual at any given time;
(2) the provision of tools and equipment, and the authority to hire and fire employees or sub-contractors;
(3) whether the manner of conducting the work is sufficiently autonomous;
(4) the degree of financial risk and whether the rewards are variable or fixed;
(5) the precise terms embodied in the agreement to conduct the work, i.e. is it a contract *of* service or contract *for* services? (see 1.4);
(6) control over the day-to-day matters such as hours of work, review and accountability;
(7) whether the individual holds himself out as being in business on his own account.

It should be noted that the Inland Revenue are paying increasingly critical attention to the distinction between the status of *employed* and *self-employed*, and are investigating in depth how this operates in practice in various areas of business.

1.6 Husband and wife

It is well known that generally in the UK husband and wife are taxed as one person, with the wife's income and capital gains being treated for this purpose as those of her husband and the husband being responsible for the payment of any taxes arising on his wife's income or gains. This whole concept has been the subject of considerable debate in recent years and in 1980 the Government issued a Green Paper setting out various alternative approaches for discussion.

As shown in Appendix A, a married man is entitled to a higher personal allowance than a single person.

In the *year of marriage*, these principles are modified as follows:

(1) for the *husband*, the married man's allowance is reduced by one-twelfth of the difference between the single and married man's allowances (£1,150 in 1984/85), for each month in the tax year which ended before his marriage (i.e. ending 5 May, 5 June, etc);

(2) for the *wife*, the single person's allowance is given to her throughout the year of marriage and the wife is not treated as married until the 6 April following the date of marriage (unless the marriage actually takes place on 6 April); thus her income is not aggregated with that of her husband during the period between the date of marriage and the following 6 April.

Where a *marriage comes to an end*, whether by separation, divorce or death, special rules also apply in the tax year concerned:

(1) the *husband* is entitled to the full married man's allowance for the year and there is no apportionment as in the year of marriage;

(2) the *wife* is in effect treated as two separate people to and from the date the marriage ends. Before that date, her income for the period is aggregated with that of her husband and their personal allowances depend on their joint circumstances; after that date, she is taxed as a single person, with the benefit of a full single person's allowance;

(3) in addition, if the marriage comes to an end because of the husband's death, the *widow* is entitled to a special personal allowance (known as 'bereavement allowance') equal to the difference between the single and married man's allowances, as an additional deduction from her income in that year and in the following tax year (provided that she has not remarried before the beginning of that later year). Again there is no apportionment.

1.7 Treatment of the wife's earned income

Except in the year of marriage (see 1.6), a wife who has earned income of her own is entitled to a further personal allowance, known as the *wife's earned income allowance*. This is currently the same as the single person's allowance, except that if the wife's earned income is insufficient to cover this allowance the balance is lost; thus it cannot be used against any of the husband's income or the wife's investment income.

If the husband's income is insufficient to cover the allowances to which he is entitled, then any excess can be used against the wife's income. Thus unutilised allowances can be passed from husband to wife but not *vice versa*.

The principle of aggregation of husband's and wife's joint incomes was substantially breached in 1971 when the concept of the *wife's earnings election* was introduced. This enables the husband and wife to elect jointly that the wife's earned income should become her own responsibility and not form part of her husband's income for tax purposes. The following particular points should be noted:

(1) the husband loses the married man's allowance and receives only the single person's allowance;
(2) the wife is in effect left in the same situation in that her wife's earned income allowance is replaced by a single person's allowance of at present the same amount;
(3) each party is entitled to the full basic rate band (up to £15,400 for 1984/85) with the higher rates being applied separately to their incomes;
(4) any investment income of the wife is not covered by the election but continues to be taxed as part of the husband's total income;
(5) the election must be made jointly by both parties, not earlier than six months before nor later than twelve months after the tax year for which it is first to apply. Thereafter it continues in operation until revoked; this must be done by both parties jointly, not later than twelve months after the end of the tax year in which the election is not to apply.

The joint earnings of the husband and wife must be substantial to make the claim worthwhile, bearing in mind

7

that the husband will forfeit part of his allowances. The precise level at which a claim is advantageous depends on the individuals' circumstances, but it should certainly be considered where the joint earnings exceed £23,000.

Example 1
The earnings of Mr Don River and his wife Sarah T. River in the year 1984/85 were as follows:

Don River	£20,000
Sarah T. River	£8,000

Without wife's earnings election tax is due as follows:

	Total £	Don £	Sarah £
Salary	28,000	20,000	8,000
Less allowances:			
Married man's allowance	(3,155)	(3,155)	
Wife's earned income allowance	(2,005)		(2,005)
	22,840	16,845	5,995
Chargeable to tax:			
at 30%	15,400	15,400	
at 40%	2,800	1,445	1,355
at 45%	4,640		4,640
	22,840	16,845	5,995
Tax due	£7,828	£5,198	£2,630

With wife's earnings election tax is due as follows:

Salary	28,000	20,000	8,000
Less single person's allowance	(4,010)	(2,005)	(2,005)
	23,990	17,995	5,995
Chargeable to tax:			
at 30%	21,395	15,400	5,995
at 40%	2,595	2,595	
	23,990	17,995	5,995
Tax due	£7,457	£5,658	£1,799
Overall tax saving	£371		

This election should not be confused with that for the *separate assessment of wife's income*, which provides a formal machinery for the division of the overall liability of husband and wife between them in ratio of their respective incomes, but does not result in any reduction in that liability.

2 Emoluments

2.1 Definition – what is included

The statutory definition of 'emoluments' is 'all salaries, fees, wages, perquisites and profits whatsoever'. This covers a very wide area and *includes* the following:

Salaries	Pensions	Holiday pay
Fees	Honoraria	Christmas boxes (in cash)
Wages	Bonuses	Pay during absence from work
Commission	Overtime pay	Payments for time spent travelling

Annuities (from approved superannuation funds)
Certain payments under the Employment Protection Act

This list is by no means comprehensive. One point which should be noted is that although salaries, etc., paid in respect of duties performed abroad are subject to deduction of tax in the normal way, there are special rules providing for a deduction from the amount assessable, depending on the number of days the employee has spent working abroad. This is dealt with in detail in Chapter 12.

There may also be a deduction available in certain circumstances for a foreign national working in the UK and this is looked at in Chapter 13.

Debts incurred by the employee and paid by the employer are treated as taxable emoluments and the amount assessed on the employee is equal to the value of the payment made by the employer.

2.2 Payments which cannot be taxed at source

The charge to tax under Schedule E arises 'in respect of emoluments *from* any office or employment'. Consequently, a gift, a benefit or other special payment made for purely personal reasons (i.e. not connected with the employee/employer relationship) cannot be taxable. Thus marriage gifts, prizes awarded to employees on passing external examinations and proceeds from benefit or testimonial matches (provided, of course, that there is no contractual entitlement) are normally tax-free. To be non-taxable, such receipts should be unexpected, entirely voluntary, non-recurring, unsolicited, not connected with the duties of the employment and of reasonable value.

There are a number of items which appear to be assessable under Schedule E but which it can be argued are not 'payments', and there are other forms of payment which simply do not lend themselves to the practical operation of PAYE. The Inland Revenue recognize the difficulties and in their publication 'Employer's Guide to PAYE', income to be included as pay is distinguished from 'income from which tax *cannot* be deducted at source' and 'income *not* to be included as pay'. Details of these are shown at Appendix E.

2.3 Concessions

By concession, the Inland Revenue do not tax certain receipts which would otherwise become taxable, namely luncheon vouchers, long service awards, and removal expenses: these are considered in more detail below.

(Payments on termination of employment, part of which may not be taxable, are dealt with in Chapter 11.)

2.3.1 *Luncheon vouchers*

Luncheon vouchers to the value of 15p per working day are not taxable. If vouchers are issued for more than 15p, the excess is taxable.

2.3.2 *Long-service awards*

Tax is not charged in respect of long-service awards provided:

(1) the award is not in cash but in the form of tangible articles of reasonable cost, including shares in the employing company or in another company in the same group, and

(2) the cost to the employer is less than £20 per year of service, and

(3) the relevant period of service is at least twenty years and no similar award has been made to the same employee in the previous ten years.

2.3.3 *Removal expenses*

If an employee incurs additional expenditure as a direct consequence of a change of residence necessitated by his employment, the employer may pay the relocation expenses on the employee's behalf. This applies to new employees as well as to those transferred to another location within the same organisation.

Besides the actual transport costs, removal expenses normally include the following:

(1) legal and survey costs, estate agent's fees and cost of any bridging loan in connection with the sale of one residence and the purchase of another;
(2) lodging and travelling expenses in looking for a suitable new residence;
(3) short-term lodging and hotel expenses if the acquisition of the new residence does not coincide with the commencement of duties at the new location;
(4) an allowance for 'settling-in' expenditure to cover necessary costs in furnishing the new residence;
(5) an allowance for 'duplication' of expenditure arising from the temporary maintenance of more than one residence;
(6) house purchase allowances where the accommodation costs in the second location are higher than in the

previous location; such an allowance may be in the form of a lump-sum payment plus a periodic payment to off-set the cost of increased mortgage payments and rates.

These expenses are not taxed *by concession* and are granted only at the Inland Revenue's discretion. All relevant circumstances are taken into account in deciding the level of tax-free allowances in individual cases and the following are basic guidelines:

   (i) costs not directly attributable to the change in locations are not allowable, e.g. the difference in price attributable to a bigger house in the second location;

  (ii) all expense allowances must be reasonable and their payment must be properly controlled;

 (iii) an allowance under (6) above should preferably take the form of decreasing payments and, in any case, must not be in the form of one lump-sum payment;

 (iv) payments under (4), (5) and (6) above are normally subject to some overriding limits in each case, each of which may be negotiated with the Inland Revenue in advance.

3 Assessing and Collecting the Tax

3.1 Introduction

The preceding sections have considered what emoluments are chargeable to tax and under what schedule the tax will be charged. The next step is to look at the system for charging and collecting the tax from each individual. This is done by assessing the chargeable emoluments for the year and setting off the personal allowances due, leaving a net taxable figure. The appropriate rates of tax are applied to this figure and the end result is the amount of tax due for the year, on the earnings of the employee. This figure is, broadly speaking, the amount the individual must pay, or has already paid, in respect of that particular year.

Before the Second World War rates of tax were low and the burden fell lightly on employees. Increased taxes during the war years brought heavier tax bills and even though these could be paid in instalments there were difficulties of collection because many employees had spent their money before the tax was due to be paid. Following unsuccessful attempts to organise deduction schemes in which the employer played a part, the Pay As You Earn system was introduced, with effect from 6 April 1944.

3.2 PAYE

This was not introduced as a new method of assessment: it was, and still is, merely a scheme for the collection of tax. Its aim is to deduct tax from each payment of emoluments, the deduction rising and falling as the pay rises and falls, so that at the end of the income tax year the tax deducted during the year is correct having regard to the employee's personal circumstances, and no further action is necessary (but see 3.5 onwards).

The backbone of the system is the 'cumulative' principle under which, as the tax year progresses, the running (cumulative) totals are kept of the amount of emoluments received from the beginning of the tax year and of the tax deducted. Each time the employer pays salaries and wages he will deduct (or refund) an amount of tax which will keep the cumulative figure deducted for each employee correct. He is supplied with tax tables by the Inland Revenue to enable him to do this on a weekly or monthly basis, whichever is appropriate.

The total of the tax deducted, less any tax refunded, for each month must be paid to the Collector of Taxes within fourteen days of the end of the month. The amount paid over also includes any national insurance contributions which may be due (see 3.9).

3.3   Coding

The amount of tax payable in a year is governed by each individual's personal circumstances and there are certain reliefs and allowances which may be claimed (see 1.1 and Appendix A). If the employer is to deduct the correct amount of tax it would seem necessary to reveal personal details about the employee to him but the Revenue are bound not to reveal to anyone the private information given to them. The difficulty is resolved by the use of codes, with a number and letter which give the employer only very limited information. In most instances it may be possible for him to deduce the marital status of a male employee but even this can be avoided if the individual so wishes.

The personal allowances and reliefs to which the individual is entitled are added together and the code resulting from this is notified to the employer. The individual is sent a notice showing all the coding allowances but the employer is only informed of the final code. There is a right of appeal against the coding notice if the individual cannot agree with allowances, etc., he is given.

Any change in personal circumstances should be notified to the Revenue in order for the code to be amended. Because of the cumulative principle involved (see 3.2) a change of code has retrospective effect to the previous 6 April. If it is increased, the tax overdeducted in previous weeks or months is refunded by the employer. If it is decreased a basis referred to as 'Week 1' or 'Month 1' is used to prevent the tax underdeducted in previous weeks or months being collected in one sum. In effect, the cumulative principle is abandoned for the year and the employer deducts tax on each pay day without reference to previous pay. The tax underdeducted prior to the date the new code is operated will have to be collected from the employee – this is dealt with at 3.5.

3.4 Deduction working sheets

The details of pay, tax and national insurance contributions are entered on a deduction working sheet which is completed by the employer on each pay day. After 5 April in each year the employer opens a new working sheet for every employee and sends the completed working sheets for the year just ended to the Collector of Taxes, with a statement on form P35 which lists the names of the employees and shows the total figure of tax deducted from each. He also provides each employee with a statement of his pay and tax for the year on a form P60.

The Collector agrees the totals, reconciles them with the remittances received from the employer during the year (see 3.2) and checks a proportion of the deduction sheets. The Department of Health and Social Security extract the information relating to national insurance contributions (see 3.9), and the sheets are then forwarded to the Inspector of Taxes office.

3.5 Assessments: underpayments and overpayments

In the normal straightforward case where the coding is correct and the employer has made the right deductions during the year, no further action should be required. Nevertheless, for a variety of reasons, too much or too little tax may be deducted during the year from the pay of a number of employees.

The Revenue will make a preliminary review of the deduction cards to eliminate the cases which are clearly in order as it is their intention to make assessments only when it is absolutely necessary to do so. In practice, an assessment is only made when after the end of the year, a repayment is due, there is a material underpayment or the employee specifically asks for it.

To expand this a little further, an assessment is not always necessary where a repayment is due, as tax relating to specific allowances can be repaid without a formal assessment. An assessment will always be made if an individual requests it but as the tax tables used by the employer (3.2) tend to underdeduct tax slightly, few would ask for an assessment unless there was a good reason for doing so.

Assessments will be made annually where there are fluctuating emoluments and the earnings basis is applied (see 3.6), and an assessment will always be made where there is an underpayment of tax for more than one year prior to the current year.

If a repayment arises (by formal assessment or not) this will be repaid to the individual but if there is an underpayment of tax this must be collected. This is commonly achieved by restricting the coding allowances for a later year although there are occasions when the underpayment will be referred to the Collector for early collection. An underpayment may be paid *voluntarily* to the Collector if this method is preferred to paying the tax due over the period of a year. Also collected through a later code number are underpayments arising because an allowance was removed from the code part-way through the tax year and there is tax to pay for the period before the code was amended (3.3). If, in any of these instances, to collect the tax in one year would cause hardship this may be spread over a period of up to three years. No action is taken to collect small amounts (normally up to £30) and a particularly lenient view is generally taken with regard to pensioners.

For instances where the earnings or accounts year basis of assessment applies (3.6.1, 3.6.2) and an underpayment arises, see 3.7.

3.6 Basis of assessment

Strictly the amount chargeable for any tax year is the amount of the 'emoluments' for that year. The majority of employees receive at the end of each week or month the amount of money which they have earned during that period. Consequently, the amount they receive in an income tax year is equal to the amount they have earned: if an assessment is necessary this will therefore be made on a 'receipts' basis.

This is not always the case however, as the amount *earned* in the year is not necessarily the same as the amount *paid* in the year. In some cases it may consist of two separate elements, i.e.:

(1) salary (fixed);

(2) commission, bonus, share of profits, etc. (variable).

If the variable element is related to the employer's accounting period as is often the case, particularly for directors where remuneration is voted at the company's annual general meeting, the amount earned is deemed to arise in that accounting period, although paid subsequently. This can result in amounts earned in one period being taxed under PAYE in a later period.

3.6.1 *Earnings basis*

The application of the *receipts basis* presents no difficulty and is used whenever possible. The earnings basis is more complicated and may cause delay in the final determination of liability.

The assessment is to be made on the earnings of the year of assessment (i.e. the year to 5 April), regardless of the date on which they are actually paid. The employer records payments on the deduction sheet on the date on which they are paid, so the assessment cannot be made using the deduction sheet figures. Payments made during the year but relating to earlier years of assessment have to be excluded from assessment in that year; likewise payments relating to that year but made in a later year have to be included. Any payments which relate to more than one tax year are apportioned to arrive at the actual amount earned in each year.

It will be seen from the following example that there will often be an underpayment of tax at the end of each tax year, due to the fact that a higher amount of emoluments is being assessed in the year than has actually been paid to the employee. For details of how this underpayment is treated, see 3.7.

Example 2

Employee receives basic salary of £5,000 per annum.

Employer's accounts are prepared to 30 June each year.

Additional fees are earned and paid as follows:

Year to 30.6.82	£ 6,000	paid 31.8.82
Year to 30.6.83	£12,000	paid 30.9.83
Year to 30.6.84	£24,000	paid 30.11.84

Deduction sheet for 1982/83 shows:	£
Salary	5,000
Fees for year to 30.6.82 (paid 31.8.82)	6,000
	£11,000

Assessable 1982/83:	
Salary	5,000
Fees: 3/12 × £ 6,000 (to 30.6.82)	1,500
9/12 × £12,000 (to 30.6.83)	9,000
	£15,500

Deduction sheet for 1983/84 shows:	
Salary	5,000
Fees for year to 30.6.83 (paid 30.9.83)	12,000
	£17,000

Assessable 1983/84	£
Salary	5,000
Fees: 3/12 × £12,000 (to 30.6.83)	3,000
9/12 × £24,000 (to 30.6.84)	18,000
	£26,000

3.6.2 *Accounts year basis*

In *earnings basis* cases the amount of remuneration assessable is computed by reference to information on the deduction sheet (details of salary) and the information shown in the employer's accounts which may be made up to any date in the year. Consequently, as mentioned above, it may be some time after the end of the income tax year before the liability can be determined.

To avoid some of this delay there is an alternative basis of assessment which, although it has no legal foundation, may nevertheless be acceptable to both the Revenue and the individual. Referred to as the *accounts year basis* of assessment, this takes the emoluments earned in the employer's accounting year as the amount assessable for the income tax year in which that accounting year ends.

For this purpose, as for the earnings basis illustrated above, a distinction may be made between a fixed element, such as a basic salary, and a variable element, such as fees or commission, which is related to the employer's accounting period.

The employee's written consent must be obtained before this basis may be applied.

Example 3
Details as for Example 2.

	£
Assessable 1982/83:	
Salary	5,000
Fees to 30.6.82	6,000
	£11,000

Assessable 1983/84	
Salary	5,000
Fees to 30.6.83	12,000
	£17,000

It will be seen that, in this particular example, the assessable amounts for both years agree with the deduction sheet figures so there should be no underpayment of tax at each 5 April. In effect, the receipts basis applies (see 3.6.1). This *only* occurs if the fees, etc. are paid in the same tax year as they are voted in the accounts. Compare the following with Example 3.

Example 4
Details as for Example 2 except that the employer prepares accounts to 31 March each year.

Fees are earned and paid as follows:

Year to 31.3.82	£ 6,000	paid 31.8.82
Year to 31.3.83	£12,000	paid 30.9.83
Year to 31.3.84	£24,000	paid 30.11.84

Deduction sheet 1983/84:	£
Salary	5,000
Fees to 31.3.83 (paid 30.9.83)	12,000
	£17,000

Assessable 1983/84:	
Salary	5,000
Fees to 31.3.84	24,000
	£29,000

An underpayment of tax will obviously arise as the amount to be assessed exceeds the amount that has been paid. For treatment of this underpayment see 3.7.

Using the accounts year basis of assessment avoids the necessity of apportioning the income for the accounting year between two income tax years. However, the Revenue always use the strict earnings basis when the income first arises or ceases – this is applied to the first year and the final two years and can apply to the second year in certain circumstances. Apart from these particular years, *whichever basis of assessment is adopted must be applied consistently*.

3.6.3 *Timing of PAYE and national insurance payments*

As indicated at the beginning of this chapter, the employer is required to account to the Collector of Taxes each month for tax deducted under PAYE and for national insurance contributions from employees. The time when this liability arises can therefore be important. This can be particularly significant when, as sometimes happens in the case of 'family' and director-controlled companies, a bonus or fee after being properly authorised is not actually paid to a director but is credited to a current account in his name in the company's books.

The general rule here is that if the net amount of the bonus or fee (i.e., after deduction of PAYE and national insurance) is credited to an account which the director is entitled to draw against as he wishes, this is regarded as constructive payment and PAYE, etc., must be computed and accounted for to the Inland Revenue accordingly. Where however the bonus or fee is authorised but only for payment at a later date, then payment for these purposes is treated as taking place at that later date (whether or not the director actually draws it then) and the liability to account to the Revenue arises accordingly.

Where the individual has drawn money from the company in advance of a prospective bonus or fee which he expects to be voted to him later, he may be effectively in the position of having borrowed money from the company at the balance sheet date. This may be regarded by the Inland Revenue as a 'beneficial loan' giving rise to tax on a benefit-in-kind (see Chapter 8); if the individual is a director of the company (as distinct from an employee) the advances may be in breach of the provisions of the Companies Acts relating to loans to directors, and the advice of the company's auditors may be required.

3.7 Unpaid emoluments

It will now be apparent from the above that assessments can include emoluments which have not actually been paid to the individual at the time the assessment is raised. The inclusion of such amounts produces an underpayment of tax but, to the extent that it relates to emoluments unpaid at 5 April, no action (but subject to the next paragraph) will be taken to collect this tax. It is carried forward to a later assessment and when the remuneration is in fact paid, tax under PAYE will be deducted, and that deduction should cover the underpayment.

There are some cases (for example directors of private companies) where the emoluments unpaid at 5 April still remain unpaid a year later. The underpayment is not then always carried forward again, but can be notified to the Collector of Taxes who takes the necessary action to collect the tax directly from the taxpayer.

3.8 Concessional repayments

It may be that, although an assessment shows an underpayment of tax because of unpaid emoluments, the individual may be entitled to a repayment in respect of an allowance or relief (e.g. mortgage interest) which was not given in the coding. Such repayment may be made by Revenue concession only. Certain limitations apply to ensure that an underpayment which is carried forward is no larger than the permitted amount and refers only to the unpaid emoluments.

3.9 National insurance contributions

Although not strictly income tax, national insurance contributions are none the less a major cost to virtually all taxpayers.

Contributions under Class 1 are payable by all employees whose earnings exceed a certain amount per week or month. The current rates (1984/85) are shown at Appendix C. Deductions are made through the PAYE system by the employer, who also makes a contribution, using tables issued by the Department of Health and Social Security ('DHSS') telling him the amount to deduct. The contributions vary depending on whether the employer is contracted in or contracted out (see Chapter 10). (If it is the latter the contributions are lower as there is no payment to the earnings-related element of the State pension scheme.)

If an individual receives a bonus or fee as a lump sum this will affect his national insurance contributions. If the amount paid to him is *less* than the total remuneration he has received for that tax year it will be added to the current salary payment and increased national insurance contributions will only be paid for that week or month. If, however, the amount paid is *greater* than the total remuneration he has received for the year, it will be spread evenly over the pay days already passed and added to each salary payment. This will then increase the contributions for each week or month accordingly, but contributions cannot be deducted from salary or bonus in excess of the maximum figure shown in the tables.

A similar situation arises where although no salary

as such is paid during the year, weekly or monthly amounts are drawn in anticipation of the final remuneration for the year when this is voted. When this latter amount is determined, it is then spread over the pay days for the year and contributions calculated accordingly.

The situations outlined above applied to all individuals before 6 April 1983, but from that date new regulations have been introduced to prevent directors reducing their national insurance liabilities by taking a low monthly salary coupled with a substantial bonus. The new rules apply to all company directors (whether employed under a contract of service or not) and state that from 6 April 1983 a director's national insurance contribution will be related to his *annual* earnings from the company in the tax year (including salary, fee and bonuses) and will be payable monthly with the PAYE tax. Any advance on account of fees will be treated in the same way, as part of his earnings. The rule concerning payment of the maximum contributions set out above still applies.

Additional points:

(1) People wishing to improve their contribution record when not working and not receiving benefit may make a voluntary contribution (currently at £4.50 per week) which will help them in qualifying for a limited range of benefits.
(2) Employees do not have to pay Class 1 contributions if they are working after the age of 65 (60 for women). The employee must supply the employer with a certificate of age exemption (obtained from the DHSS) to excuse him from making the deductions.

(3) Married women at one time were given the opportunity of paying reduced contributions under Class 1. The employer must be presented with a certificate of reduced liability. This arrangement has now been closed and no new certificates are being issued.

(4) People with more than one job may pay excessive contributions during the tax year. It is possible to claim a refund and the DHSS publish leaflets explaining the procedure to follow.

(5) Individuals who are employees but who are also self-employed will be liable to pay contributions under Class 1, Class 2 and possibly Class 4. Any excess paid will generally be refunded. Payments of Class 2 and Class 4 contributions may be deferred until after the end of the tax year, which avoids the need for a refund.

(6) The DHSS publish leaflets which give guidance on national insurance matters to people in varying circumstances, to help them determine the amount of contributions to be paid.

3.10 PAYE audit

The Inland Revenue have always had the power to inspect an employer's records to satisfy themselves that PAYE is being properly applied against salaries and wages.

In recent years, with the increase in the provision of benefits of all kinds to employees, the Revenue have considerably increased the scope of their examinations in this area (known as 'PAYE audits'). They now have about 700 specialist staff engaged on this work in the field and the intention is that all employers' records will be examined every 3–5 years. These audit teams mainly concentrate on the payment of allowances, expenses and other cash items which may give rise to a liability to account for PAYE tax and also in appropriate circumstances to national insurance contributions.

The Revenue are also giving increased attention to the tax treatment of non-cash benefits; the examination of these is normally dealt with by local Inspectors of Taxes.

How these examinations are carried out by the Revenue and their consequences for employers and employees are outside the scope of this book. Suffice it to say that any employer who is subject to one of these investigations may be well advised to consider obtaining professional advice and assistance!

4 Expenses

4.1 Allowable deductions

The legislation states that tax shall be charged on the full emoluments from an office or employment 'subject to such deductions only as may be authorised by the Taxes Act ....' A deduction is therefore only possible if it is expressly allowed by statute (4.5) or is incurred *wholly, exclusively and necessarily in the performance of the duties* of that employment'. The words in italics are crucial in establishing a claim and are looked at in more detail below.

4.2 'Wholly and exclusively'

The words appear stringent and exacting but they are interpreted by the Revenue in a practical rather than a literal sense. In some instances, therefore, an allowance is not excluded simply because the total amount incurred does not qualify. If part of an expense can be related to what is necessary (4.3) in the performance of the duties

(4.4) but the expense as a whole is not wholly and exclusively incurred for that reason, the part which does so qualify is admitted as a deduction.

An example of this is the use of a room at home as an office by an employee who is obliged to work at home to perform his duties. An appropriate proportion of the total house expenses would be admitted. In general, an individual's dwelling house is exempt from capital gains tax when it is sold if it has been the only or main private residence during the period of ownership. If it is established that part of the property has been used *exclusively* for business purposes the capital gains tax exemption may be lost on that part of the property. This problem can be avoided if the room is also used for private purposes.

Where it is not possible to divide an expense between business and private use, the expense cannot qualify under the 'wholly and exclusively' rule and the entire amount is therefore lost. This is the reason why, for instance, people who wear suits for work cannot obtain any deduction for the cost – the suits can also be worn for private purposes. This point was borne out in a case where a computer engineer had to wear a suit for work, even though it got damaged due to his having to carry out repair work while wearing it! The position is different where special protective clothing has to be worn, e.g. goggles worn by a welder (see 4.6).

4.3 'Necessarily'

An expense is 'necessarily' incurred only if an employee is obliged to incur that expense in the performance of his duties. To be 'necessary' the expense must be 'reasonable' taking into account the status of the employee and the primary purpose of the expenditure. For instance, the cost of the hiring of a Rolls-Royce by a post-room employee to deliver documents around the Home Counties is unlikely to satisfy this test.

It is sometimes difficult to make a distinction between an imposition set by the employee's duties (which is allowable) and an imposition set by the employer (which is not necessarily allowable). In practice, it is normally only when a particular type of expense is brought to the attention of the Inland Revenue by an employee seeking to claim costs over and above those allowed by the employer that the distinction has to be made.

Any taxpayer contemplating expenditure which is likely to be challenged by the Inland Revenue because it is not 'necessary' should consider what evidence can be put forward for a successful claim. If possible, board minutes should be made available to authorise specific expenditure; alternatively a formal memorandum (or letter) from the employer may be helpful. It must be recognised that the Revenue (with the support of the courts) do interpret these provisions very stringently, and the production of evidence of the kind mentioned may still not be conclusive.

With regard to *travelling expenses* see 4.8 below.

4.4   'In the performance of . . .'

The fact that an expense may be relevant to the employment is not sufficient for it to be an allowable deduction. It must be necessarily incurred in the performance of the duties of that employment. As an example, compare two teachers of mathematics. The first purchases books with the intention of keeping his own knowledge up to date. The other is obliged, under the terms of his employment, to purchase books which he requires as part of his teaching in the classroom. The first claim would be disallowed; the second claim would be allowed as the expenditure was incurred in the performance of the duties.

4.5 Expenses specifically allowed by statute

The following expenses are deductible in full irrespective of whether paid by employee or employer:

(1) contributions to approved pension schemes and under annuity contracts (see Chapter 10);
(2) membership subscriptions (but not entrance fees) to approved professional bodies (see 4.9);
(3) capital allowances in respect of capital equipment used in the course of the duties of the employment;
(4) interest on specific loans (but not overdrafts) to finance the purchase of capital equipment qualifying for capital allowances as in (3) above, used in the course of the duties of the employment, but only for interest paid not more than three years after the end of the tax year in which the loan is taken out.

4.6 Flat-rate expenses

Flat-rate deductions for expenses covering most classes of manual labour have been agreed with the trade unions concerned. If these are claimed they will be allowed without further enquiry. The existence of an agreed flat-rate deduction does not preclude the employee from claiming in respect of the actual expense incurred, although the Revenue would be unlikely to admit a larger claim.

4.7 Business entertaining expenses

Statute provides that any expenditure incurred in entertaining overseas customers (strictly defined) can be treated as allowable. Any other entertaining is disallowed either in computing the employer's tax liability *or* in computing the employee's tax liability. Depending on whether the employee pays tax at a higher rate than the employer, the following guidelines should be followed to achieve the optimum position:

(1) *specific reimbursements* of actual entertaining expenditure incurred by an employee would enable the employer to identify the expenditure, and provided that is disallowed in computing the employer's tax liability it should qualify as a deductible expense as regards the employee, subject always to satisfying the 'wholly and exclusively' test (see 4.2);

(2) entertaining expenditure met by the employee out of *his gross pay* or out of *round-sum expense allowances* (see 4.10) will be deductible in computing the employer's tax liability; consequently the employee cannot claim a deduction.

It should be noted that the rule under (2) may have adverse tax consequences for the employees of organisations not taxable in the UK (e.g. the representative offices of overseas companies which are not taxable here) because such employers cannot suffer any disallowance and this therefore has to fall on the employees irrespective of the method of payment.

Generally, reasonable costs for staff entertainment are not assessed on an employee or director.

4.8 Travelling expenses

Travelling expenditure between two locations during the course of one employment is normally allowable. By concession, this rule is extended for application to the expenses of travelling between different locations in the course of employment duties for other companies in the same group. This concession can be of particular benefit to an individual who is director of a number of group companies.

Travelling expenses from home to a place of employment are *not* regarded as 'necessary' because generally the duties of the employment only commence when the employee reaches his place of employment; where he lives is a matter of personal choice. This position may be modified where it can be shown that the employee is *required* to work from his own house and not from his employer's place of business; this could apply for example to a representative who covers an area centred on his house and who only makes occasional visits to his employer's office.

In spite of this, it is possible for employers to provide for travelling expenses of employees between home and work in certain circumstances.

Where an employee is required to work away from his main place of employment, the travelling expenses from the main place of employment to the site of work are allowable. If the employee travels direct from home to the site it may also be possible to claim these travelling expenses as allowable. A deduction may also be allowed for expenses incurred in additional travel from home to work outside normal working hours; for example, for a teacher to attend a parents' meeting at the school during the evening.

Once the necessity of a travelling expense has been proved, it is allowable even if the employee derives other advantages from his travel, i.e. the expense need *not* be 'wholly and exclusively' for the purposes of the employment duties. For instance, an employee's travelling costs from his place of employment (outside London) to London will not be disallowed if, having worked a full day in London, he visits the London Palladium before travelling home. Special considerations may apply in the case of an individual with an overseas employment (see 12.12) or of a foreign national working in the UK (see 13.6.1).

4.9 Subscriptions

Subscriptions paid to professional institutions are allowable as deductions if membership is a condition of the employment or if the institution's activities are *directly* relevant to the employment. The Revenue has published a list of approved professional bodies and learned societies and this shows the agreed amount of the allowable subscriptions.

If the employer is liable to pay such subscriptions directly (e.g. under the contract of employment) there will be a taxable benefit on the employee in the case of directors and higher-paid employees (see 5.3). It is the employee's responsibility to claim a deduction if the expense qualifies under the normal rules.

Club membership subscriptions are, in general, not allowable under these provisions.

4.10   Round-sum allowances

If the employer pays a round-sum allowance to cover all expenses he considers the employee may incur in the performance of his duties, the employee is taxable on the amount received, subject to a claim for specific expenses he has incurred. Any claim made in this respect will have to meet the stringent tests of being 'wholly, exclusively and necessarily' incurred as described in 4.2 and 4.3 above.

4.11   Other expenses – general notes

These can include such items as subsistence, hotel and incidental living expenses, and travelling expenses other than those for the employee himself. The same criteria as set out in 4.1 still apply in order for the expense to be allowable.

In practical terms this empowers the Inland Revenue to disallow expenses which are identifiable as additional to the primary purpose. For instance, an employee travels from his normal place of employment in Glasgow to London for employment duties on a Tuesday and his assignment is completed by Friday. Instead of returning to Glasgow on Friday, he stays in London and returns on Monday morning. The hotel and incidental costs *for the weekend* will be disallowed, though as seen in 4.8 this will not affect the deductibility of the fare back to Glasgow.

Travelling and board and lodging expenses of an employee's wife accompanying him to a location away from the normal place of employment often fail the 'necessity' test (see 4.3). Several factors may assist in sustaining its deductibility. Sometimes the wife may possess technical expertise (such as a formal qualification or by way of experience) which can be argued to be necessary for the husband in performing his duties; sometimes an employee's health is such as to require the attention of his wife accompanying him. Other factors being equal, the case may be stronger if an employee is accompanied by his daughter (or other relative) rather than by his wife. In appropriate circumstances it may be possible to claim that the presence of the wife was essential for business-entertainment purposes; in such cases, there is a stronger presumption that her presence was not 'necessary' and the Inland Revenue will require full details of the nature and extent of business entertaining. As regards the expenditure incurred by a wife the tests set out in 4.2 to 4.4 are construed very strictly.

Although less usual, exactly the same considerations apply where the *wife* is the employee and she is accompanied by her *husband* on a business trip.

5 Fringe Benefits – Basic Rules

5.1 Introduction

The broad effect of the legislation is that, in the cases to which it applies, expenses payments and the value of benefits are assessed under Schedule E on the director or employee, leaving him to claim any deduction which may be due for expenses necessarily incurred in the performance of the duties of the office or employment (Chapter 4).

Many employers give their employees 'benefits' or 'perquisites' of some description. The majority of these 'fringe benefits', as they are called, are taxable and the present Government has introduced legislation designed to discourage growth in this area by bringing an increasing number of benefits effectively into the tax net.

This chapter covers the general rules for the taxing of fringe benefits and Chapter 6 deals with specific items in the legislation.

5.2   Salary or benefit?

There are various ways in which an employee can receive a benefit from his employer: because of the method of taxing fringe benefits it is marginally better for the employee to receive a benefit and pay tax on it than it is to receive extra salary in the same amount. The following example shows the tax implications of varying ways of giving an employee a benefit, and the cost to both employee and employer.

Example 5
Mr W. Asher is an employee who pays tax at the basic rate of 30 per cent. He is employed by a company Clene Ltd which pays corporation tax at 45 per cent. Mr A wishes to acquire a washing machine costing £400.

The alternatives (ignoring national insurance) are:

(1) if Mr A buys the washing machine out of his own net income it will cost him £400. It will cost C Ltd nothing;
(2) if C Ltd pays Mr A extra salary of £400 to enable him to buy the washing machine, he will have to contribute £120 to the cost:

	£
Gross salary payment	400
Less tax at 30%	120
Net payment to Mr A	£280

	£
The cost to the company is £220:	
Payment to Mr A	400
Less tax relief at 45%	180
Net cost to company	£220

(3) if C Ltd wishes to pay Mr A sufficient salary to enable him to purchase the machine at no cost to himself, it is necessary to pay £571:

Gross salary payment	571
Less tax at 30%	171
Net payment to Mr A	£400

The cost to the company is £314:	
Payment to Mr A	571
Less tax relief at 45%	257
Net cost to company	£314

(4) If C Ltd gives the washing machine to Mr A this constitutes a taxable benefit on him of £400: tax due on this, at 30 per cent, is £120, which he will have to bear. The cost to the company is £220 (as in (2) above).

Comparing (2) and (4) above the figures are identical but in addition to the tax of £120, if method (2) was used Mr Asher may also have to pay national insurance contributions on the extra salary of £400. A further difference is that the tax would be deducted from the salary when it is paid and Mr Asher would have to find the balance to purchase the washing machine. On the other hand, if he is to be taxed on a benefit this will be assessed after 5 April and the tax would be collected over a whole tax year by restricting his coding allowances (3.3) thus avoiding the necessity for any capital outlay.

5.3 Who falls to be taxed?

There are some benefits which are taxable on all employees whatever their status or salary but the greater part of the legislation applies to 'directors and higher-paid employees'.

In general terms the definition includes all company directors (in the case of a company managed by members, each member is a 'director' for this purpose), and all employees whose remuneration is at the rate of £8500 or more per annum (see 5.4).

A full-time working director who, together with his associates (relatives, partners, etc.), controls less than 5 per cent of the ordinary share capital, is excluded from the definition of 'director' but can still, of course, be included as a higher-paid employee.

This definition is fundamental to the understanding of the taxation of fringe benefits because there are quite distinct rules for valuing the benefits provided by reason of the employment, depending on the category in which an individual falls to be taxed.

5.4 The £8500 threshold

'Remuneration' for this purpose is defined to include:
(a) all salaries, wages, etc., as generally understood;

(b) the value of all benefits received as if the employee were 'higher paid';

(c) all expenses reimbursed to the employee *before* any deduction is made for those expenses which are deductible under the 'wholly, exclusively and necessarily incurred' provisions (see Chapter 4).

If, after taking these ingredients into account, the individual's total 'remuneration' is still less than £8500, the benefits included under (b) will not be brought into charge to tax (unless of course they are such as to be taxable in any event).

It should also be noted that the inclusion of items under (c) for this particular purpose does not mean that such expenses are to be treated any differently for tax purposes generally: the employee is still entitled to claim the appropriate deduction if this meets the tests set out in Chapter 4.

5.5 Valuing benefits – directors and higher-paid employees

Apart from certain benefits (provision of cars, beneficial loan arrangements and share incentive schemes – see Chapters 7, 8 and 9 respectively) the general rule is that for tax purposes the value to be placed on a benefit provided for a director/higher-paid employee is the 'cash equivalent' or 'cost' of the benefit. This is the actual expense incurred by the employer in providing the benefit, less so much of that expense as is made good by the individual to the employer.

If the benefit is the use of an asset owned by the employer, the cash equivalent is the 'annual value' of the asset. This is calculated as 20 per cent of the market value of the asset when it was first used to provide a benefit. Where an asset was first used to provide a benefit before 6 April 1980 the annual value is taken as 10 per cent of its market value when first applied as a benefit. (Cars are *not* treated in this way – see Chapter 7.)

Where an asset is transferred from the employer to the individual, being a director or higher-paid employee, and the asset has already been available for his use, the measure of the benefit is the market value of the asset at the date that it was first put at his disposal, less the amount on which he has already been taxed as a benefit in kind for his use of it before transfer to him.

Thus in Example 5 if Clene Ltd continued to own the washing machine but made the use of it available to Mr A at no cost to him, his benefit would be limited to 20 per cent of £400, i.e. £80.

Example 6
On 6 April 1982 Mr G. Ainer was provided by his employer with the use of new furniture costing £10,000 in his flat. In June 1984 the employer hands the furniture over to Mr Ainer free of charge: its market value is then £3000.

Market value at date asset made available to Mr A's use (i.e. cost)	£10,000
Benefit in kind 1982/83 20% of £10,000	£ 2,000
Benefit in kind 1983/84 20% of £10,000	£ 2,000
Benefit in kind 1984/85 £10,000 − (£2,000 + £2,000)	£ 6,000

(The market value at the date of transfer is irrelevant.)

46

Where an asset in question is hired, leased or rented by the person providing it, the 'annual value' as computed above would be replaced by the cost of hire (or lease or rent) if that produced a higher figure. For the unwary this rule can have adverse tax consequences if an employer should hire expensive assets for use by employees.

Any payment or fringe benefit provided to a director/higher-paid employee or for members of his family (spouse, children, children's spouses, servants, dependents and 'guests') by his employer is deemed to be so provided by reason of his employment. (This rule does not apply to a payment or a fringe benefit provided by an employer, being an *individual*, in the normal course of a domestic, family or personal relationship.) Benefits provided to directors or higher-paid employees by *other parties* must be shown to be received by reason of the employment, if they are to be taxable.

If a director/higher-paid employee and a member of his family were employed by the same employer, it is technically possible for the individual to be charged to tax as regards payments or benefits provided to himself *and* the member of his family. However it is considered unlikely that the Inland Revenue would take this point in practice, if the member of the family is a bona-fide employee.

5.6 Valuing benefits – employees earning less than £8500

It was mentioned above (see 5.3) that some benefits are taxable on all employees whatever their salary or status and these are dealt with separately (see Chapter 6). The basic rule for an employee earning *less* than £8500 per annum is that he can only be taxed on a benefit if it is money's worth and convertible by him into money, and if so he is taxed on the 'net realisable value', i.e. the second-hand value. Also, to be taxable, the benefit must be received as *remuneration for services rendered* in the employment. The fact that someone receiving a benefit is an employee does not *of itself* prove that what he receives is a taxable benefit from his employment. This is something of a grey area, and professional advice should always be sought in cases of doubt. An example of a 'benefit' which would not be taxable would be a prize received in a raffle which is only open to employees.

Such employees can be put in an advantageous tax position by e.g. allowing them the use of company-owned assets which depreciate rapidly and then selling the assets to them at that depreciated value, paying school fees in respect of their children (14.7) and providing employer-administered in-house pension facilities (see 10.8).

It is essential that the provision of such benefits is *contractually undertaken and paid for* by the employer. For instance, the employer should place the order for, say, a new car, accept delivery and negotiate the terms of purchase before selling it after a period of use to the employee at the depreciated price. If this is not done, the Inland Revenue might successfully contend that the payment by the employer represented the discharge of the employee's debt and assess the employee for the price of the new car (see 2.1). It is also necessary for the payment to be made *direct by the employer*. If an employee is merely reimbursed for such expenditure, the sums reimbursed will form part of the employee's taxable emoluments subject of course to any deductions available to the employee under the general rules (see Chapter 4).

5.7 Returns and dispensations

Every employer is required to notify to the Inland Revenue details of all benefits, expense payments and allowances provided to each director/higher-paid employee in each tax year. This is done by completing a form P11D in respect of each person. To save time and administration costs for all concerned, the employer may apply for a dispensation from having to include routine expense payments and benefits on forms P11D. For this purpose, the employer must satisfy the Inspector that all the benefits and expenses will be covered by an equivalent amount of expense deductions. Because this requirement is applied strictly, only *routine* travelling, subsistence and hotel expenses are normally included in applications for dispensation.

Where a dispensation is given, the relevant expenses need not be included in forms P11D nor in the income tax returns of employees. They are also ignored for the purposes of deciding whether or not an employee is over the £8500 limit (see 5.4). It should be noted however that a dispensation will not normally be granted where it has the effect of moving an employee from the 'higher-paid' bracket to the category of an employee earning less than £8500 so as to render certain benefits, e.g. use of a company car, no longer subject to tax.

6 Fringe Benefits – Specific legislation

6.1 Taxable benefits – summary chart

Table 6.1 sets out various fringe benefits and whether or not they are taxable. However, this list does not necessarily cover all the various forms of benefit which may be provided by an employer.

TABLE 6.1   Taxable Benefits

Benefit	Directors and employees earning over £8500 per annum	Employees earning less than £8500 per annum
Holidays	Taxable in full, unless combined with a business trip, when the 'holiday element' may still be taxable	Not taxable, providing employer pays direct and does not reimburse employee
Transport vouchers/season tickets (e.g. British Rail)	Taxable	Up to 5 April 1982 not taxable subject to certain conditions (see 6.2). Taxable from 6 April 1982

Table 6.1 (*continued*)

Benefit	Directors and employees earning over £8500 per annum	Employees earning less than £8500 per annum
Suggestion scheme payment	Not taxable provided amount is reasonable and not a term of contract	Same as directors
Prize incentive schemes	Taxable	Taxable
Examination prizes	Not taxable (as for suggestion schemes)	Same as directors
Canteen facilities	Not taxable, provided available in one form or another to *all* staff	Not taxable
Luncheon vouchers	Not taxable providing not in excess of 15p per day (see 2.3.1)	Same as directors
Seminars/ external courses/ conferences	Not generally taxable if borne and paid for by employer	Not taxable
Medical insurance	Taxable – on cost to employer. If taken out for group of employees, each is taxable on a proportion of the cost. *Not* taxable if insurance is against the cost of medical treatment abroad where the need arises whilst employee is performing his duties outside UK. N.B. Applies only to medical *insurance*. Provision of medical *treatment* – benefit is computed in accordance with general rules (see Chapter 5)	Up to 5 April 1982 taxable on cost to employer. Not taxable from 6 April 1982.

Table 6.1 (*continued*)

Benefit	Directors and employees earning over £8500 per annum	Employees earning less than £8500 per annum
Welfare, sports and social facilities	Not taxable	Not taxable
Transfer of company-owned assets to employees, e.g. yacht, furniture, living accommodation	Taxable on market value at time first made available to director/ employee less benefit already charged on him (see 5.5)	Taxable on market value at time of transfer
Use of furniture or clothing, etc., owned by employer	Taxable on 20% of the value when use commences (see 5.5)	Not taxable
Credit cards	Taxable from 6 April 1982 (see 6.2)	Same as directors
Scholarships awarded to employers' children	Taxable on payments made after 15 March 1983 (see 14.7)	Not taxable

6.2 Vouchers

The taxation of vouchers provided by the employer is dependent on whether they are 'cash' or 'non-cash' vouchers.

A *cash voucher* means any voucher, stamp or similar document capable of being exchanged (whether singly or together with other such documents) for a sum of money greater than, equal to, or not substantially less than the expense incurred in providing the voucher by the person who provides it. (It does not matter if it can also be exchanged for goods and services.) It does not include a document intended for a person to obtain payment of a sum which would not be taxable under Schedule E.

A *non-cash voucher* is more difficult to define. It does not include a cash voucher but, subject to that, means any voucher, stamp or similar document capable of being exchanged (again whether singly or together with other such documents) for money, goods or services (or a combination of the three).

With effect from 6 April 1982, the definition of non-cash voucher is extended to include a so-called *cheque voucher*, which is defined as a cheque provided for an employee which he may use for payment for particular goods or services.

Precisely what constitutes a non-cash voucher as distinct from a cash voucher may well have to be decided by the courts in due course but it is unlikely to be significant in practice. If employers wish to ensure that employees are not caught by the taxing provisions they should as far as possible avoid issuing pieces of paper!

The legislation sets out to apply to tax the exchangeable value of a cash voucher and does not in practice change the assessable position of what is in any event a taxable emolument. Any employee receiving a non-cash voucher is deemed to have received an emolument equal to the expense incurred in providing the voucher and the money, goods or services for which it is capable of being exchanged.

Provisions introduced in the 1981 Finance Act and refined in the 1982 Act were aimed at clarifying the definitions of *credit cards* and *transport vouchers* so as to ensure that these are within the scope of the legislation. A 'credit card' is defined for tax purposes as including ordinary credit cards, charge cards, cards giving access to bank cash points, retailers' own credit cards, cards designed to facilitate the purchase of specified goods or services and generally any card which enables an employee to obtain money, goods or services leaving his employer (or some other person) to pay the bill. Specifically excluded are discount cards issued by employers to their employees enabling them to buy goods from their employer at less than normal retail value.

As a practical concession, because this could involve the apportionment of trivial amounts, the subscription and interest charges made by credit card companies are not included as 'expenses' for this purpose.

A 'transport voucher' is defined as a ticket, pass or other document intended to enable the possessor to obtain passenger transport services, but *excluding* a voucher provided for an employee of a passenger-transport undertaking under arrangements in operation on 25 March 1982.

6.3 Living accommodation

(1) Where an employee is provided with living accommodation by his employer, the employee is liable to tax on the value of the accommodation provided. The rules apply whether or not the employee is a director

or higher-paid employee, and are designed to tax the use of employer-owned accommodation and any other associated benefits such as the use of furniture, payments for electricity, gas, cleaning and upkeep costs. Any costs incurred by the employer in his capacity as the legal owner are not normally taxable. These include structural repairs, maintenance costs and insurance. The position concerning rates is discussed separately (see 6.3.1)

(2) The benefits arising from the use of accommodation is the gross *rateable* value rather than the open market *rental*. The former is usually considerably lower than the latter and offers scope for conferring a benefit which will not be taxable at its true value. If the accommodation provided to the employee is his only residence, the capital gains tax exemption for an individual's only or main residence will not be available on the house. If the accommodation is leased or rented by the employer, the taxable benefit is the higher of the rent payable and the gross rateable value

(3) *With effect from 6 April 1984* an additional benefit is charged where the accommodation costs the employer (or any person 'connected' with him) more than £75,000, and operates to impose in addition to the amount in (2) a charge on the excess over £75,000 equivalent to the 'official' rate of interest applied to beneficial loans (at present 12 per cent – see Chapter 8). For this purpose, 'cost' covers expenditure incurred in acquiring the property and on improvements prior to the tax year for which the benefit is being assessed. Where the employee first occupies the property after 30 March 1983

and it was acquired by the employer (or a connected person) more than six years before the date of first occupation, market value at the latter date is taken as 'cost'.

(4) The annual use value is not taxable if the employee is in 'representative occupation', i.e. if he is required to reside in the accommodation either:

(a) for the proper performance of his employment duties (e.g. a caretaker), or

(b) for the better performance of his employment duties and it is customary to provide such accommodation in the particular type of employment (e.g. a bank manager), or

(c) as part of special security arrangements (e.g. a civil servant assigned to Northern Ireland).

Categories (a) and (b) are not available to directors of the employer company or of its associated companies, unless they are full-time working directors owning less than 5 per cent of the share capital, or they own less than 5 per cent of the share capital and the company is non-profitmaking. As regards directors and higher-paid employees in representative occupation see 6.3.2.

(5) Running costs such as electricity, gas, telephone, etc., are normally regarded as contractually incurred by the employee so that if discharged by the employer, they will be taxable in full subject to a claim for expenses incurred wholly, exclusively and necessarily in the course of performing the employment duties.

(6) Where the employer provides furniture or other assets for use by the employee, additional benefit will arise in accordance with the general rules concerning employer-owned assets (see 5.5).

(7) Where employer-owned accommodation has been occupied by an employee under such circumstances as to entitle the employee to protection under specific legislation concerning tenancies, the market value of the property subject to that tenancy may be considerably less than the true open market value. Detailed professional advice is essential at the outset on such matters as valuations and the legal and tax implications of certain categories of tenancies. Subject to this, there is considerable scope for an employer to provide a non-taxable benefit to an employee by purchasing property, creating a protected tenancy and transferring the ownership after the market value has depreciated because of the tenancy.

(8) Where the employee pays rent to his employer for the use of the accommodation etc., this amount is deducted from the benefit in arriving at the amount taxable on him.

6.3.1 *Occupier for rating purposes*

The General Rate Act 1967, section 16, states that the rating authority is required to *rate the occupier of every property*. This does not apply in the case of 'representative occupation' (see 6.3 (4)) where the employer is treated as the occupier and is charged the rates accordingly even though it is the employee who actually lives in the property. If this is the case, there is no taxable benefit on the employee even if the cost is borne by the employer.

In general the law is interpreted literally and the person actually occupying the property is treated as the occupier for rating purposes. In the instance of an employer providing living accommodation for an employee simply because he had nowhere else to live, the employee would therefore be treated as the occupier.

If the employee is treated as the occupier for rating purposes, payments for rates would be employee debts discharged by the employer, and the assessable benefit will be the sum total of the amounts so discharged (see 2.1).

6.3.2 *Representative occupation for director/higher-paid employees*

Directors and higher-paid employees who live in representative occupation, as defined in 6.3 (4), will be taxed on a benefit arising from the use of furniture and effects, plus repair, maintenance, decoration, heating, lighting and cleaning costs borne by the employer. The benefit is limited to 10 per cent of the individual's emoluments.

Example 7
Astute Ltd incurs the following expenditure in providing its executive Mr A Fiddler with the use of a London flat for the year to 5 April 1985:

Flat purchased for £150,000 (rateable value £3,000 p.a.) on 5 April 1984.
Furniture and effects purchased for £20,000 on 5 April 1984.

Expenses paid by Astute Ltd in year to 5 April 1985:

	£
Gas and electricity	1,400
Repairs	800
Upkeep of garden	1,800
Rates	2,400

Mr Fiddler's emoluments for the year to 5 April 1985 are £50,000 after deduction of allowable expenses and contributions to an approved pension scheme. He pays £2,000 p.a. rent to Astute Ltd for this accommodation.

The taxable benefit is computed as follows:

		£
(1)	Use of accommodation rateable value 3,000 + rates 2,400	5,400
	additional charge 12% of (150,000–75,000)	9,000
(2)	Use of furniture (20% of £20,000)	4,000
(3)	Expenses – gas, etc.	1,400
	– repairs	800
	– upkeep of garden	1,800
		22,400
	Less rent paid	2,000
	Assessable 1984/85	£20,400

If 'representative occupation' established (6.3(3)) benefit is limited to 10 per cent of £50,000, i.e. £5,000 less rent paid £2,000, this gives a net charge to tax on £3,000.

6.4 Director's PAYE

With effect from 6 April 1983, where a company pays remuneration to a director without deducting the right amount of PAYE tax and subsequently accounts for that (correct) amount to the Revenue, any excess over the amount deducted from the director's pay is to be assessed on him as a benefit.

This provision does not apply to a higher paid *employee*, nor to a full-time working director, who (with his associates) controls less than 5 per cent of the company's ordinary share capital; this latter category is generally excluded from the term 'director', as mentioned in 5.3 above.

7 The Company Car

7.1 Introduction

The object of the legislation concerning company cars is to tax an individual on the benefit he derives from having a company car available for his own use. Several years ago the Inland Revenue formed the view that it was imposs- ible to ensure that all individuals who had a company car paid the correct amount of tax appropriate to the benefit attributable to the car. Legislation introduced in 1976 therefore sought to simplify the assessment procedure, while at the same time endeavouring to find a more efficient system, by introducing the concept of flat-rate benefits, almost regardless of the private use made of the car. There have been changes in the scheme since its introduction and for the sake of simplicity only the current provisions are dealt with in this section.

The legislation only applies to directors and higher-paid employees (5.3) but it is interesting to take note of a case that went through the courts several years ago. It concerned an employee who was not a director or higher-paid employee but who was given the opportunity of having a company car, the arrangement being that he took a reduction in wages related to the age and type of the car. The Revenue sought to assess him on the reduction in salary as they claimed that this was also part of his emoluments. It was decided that the free use of a car for his own purposes was a perk, in respect of which he was chargeable to income tax under Schedule E, because if he had chosen to forego it he could have received a higher cash salary instead. The full amount of the perk was held to be the sum of money which he could have received had he chosen to forego the chance of the company car.

It should also be noted that the cost of providing a chauffeur is *always* treated as additional to the cost of providing a company car.

7.2 'Table' benefits

The benefit is decided by reference to the age, cost and cylinder capacity of the car according to a table laid down for each tax year. The scale rates at present fixed for 1984/85 are shown at Appendix D; these rates can be changed at any time by Statutory Instrument.

An individual whose car falls into the category of 'insubstantial business use' will be taxed on 1.5 times the normal scale rate. This use is defined as business mileage in the year of less than 2500 miles.

Where an individual is taxable on two (or more) cars made available concurrently, the taxable amount is again increased to 1.5 times the normal scale rate, for each car other than the one used to the greatest extent for the employee's business travel.

It is possible to claim a reduction of the taxable charge to one-half of the prescribed scale rates if business mileage exceeds 18,000 miles in the year.

Where the car is not made available to the employee until part-way through the tax year or it is incapable of being used throughout a period of not less than thirty consecutive days, the flat-rate benefit will be reduced on a time-apportionment basis.

The taxable benefit covers all expenses incurred *directly* by the employer and no further taxable benefit will arise as regards the private-use proportion of such expenses. As regards expenses paid by the employee and subsequently reimbursed by the employer, the employer will be treated as having discharged an employee's debt (see 2.1) and the full amount of sums reimbursed (less the appropriate proportion of business usage) will be treated as a taxable benefit in addition to the fixed scale benefit. To obtain maximum advantage, therefore, steps should be taken to ensure that all car expenses are the legal liability of, and are directly paid for by, the employer.

As with most fringe benefits, any contribution by the employee towards the cost to the employer of providing a car will be deducted from the table benefit. As a general rule, the employee and employer should benefit by not requiring such contributions from employees and keeping the salaries at correspondingly reduced figures. This is because cash contributions from employees would generally be regarded as being in respect of a taxable supply (for VAT purposes) made by the employer and the employee will have made the contributions from his net (i.e. after-tax) income. However, if the employee is given the *choice* of not making a cash contribution and taking a corresponding reduction in his emoluments, the Inland Revenue could successfully argue that the reduction in salary was itself an assessable benefit (see note on case referred to in 7.1 above).

7.3 'Pool' cars

No benefit will arise on the use of a company car if it can be proved that the car is a 'pool' car. The conditions for this are as follows:

(1) the car is actually used by two or more employees (hence the term 'pool');
(2) any non-business use of the car is purely incidental;
(3) the car is not normally kept overnight on or near an employee's residence.

To prevent abuse, the Revenue insist that these three requirements must be strictly adhered to.

7.4 Petrol

When the legislation relating to the taxation of car benefits was introduced in 1976, the position regarding petrol supplied by the employer was not dealt with effectively. In particular an employee having the use of a company car could find himself in a quite different tax position depending on whether he was reimbursed by his employer for the cost of the petrol or the employer paid the garage direct for the petrol. The former would give rise to a taxable benefit under the general rules relating to reimbursed expenses but the latter would not give rise to a benefit at all.

The position regarding credit cards was also unsatisfactory, in that it was not clear whether payment by means of a company credit card used by an employee, was the equivalent of a 'reimbursement' or a 'direct payment'.

It was considered that this uncertain state of affairs was leading to some abuse and legislation was introduced in the Finance Act 1981 to overcome the problem. As with the car benefit legislation generally, the new provisions apply only to directors and higher-paid employees (5.3).

The legislation provides that where fuel is provided for a car made available to a director or higher-paid employee, he is to be treated as having received an emolument equal to the 'cash equivalent' of that benefit. This is to be determined by reference to a table of scale benefits, dependent on the size of the car, similar in principle to that already in operation for all car benefits described above (see 7.2) with adjustments for high business use, etc.

The cash equivalent is reduced to nil in any year if the employee is required to reimburse the cost of the fuel provided for private use *and* does so, or if fuel is made available *only* for business use. It would seem that no reduction in the cash equivalent is made if the employee is only required to reimburse a proportion of the cost or if he makes a voluntary contribution towards the cost. In the light of this, where an employee does make some reimbursement or contribution to his employer for private use, this should, as far as possible, be attributed to his use of the car as such, thus reducing the corresponding cash equivalent, rather than towards the cost of private petrol, with no analogous reduction.

The scale rates for 1984/85 are shown at Appendix D.

In the meantime, new provisions relating to credit cards described in 6.2 became operative on 6 April 1982. From that date, all directors and employees, whether higher-paid or not, who are able to purchase petrol for private use, whether the cost of this is reimbursed by the employer or is met by means of a company credit card, will be taxed on that cost (unless they reimburse the cost to their employer). Employers will therefore need to include the requisite information in their returns of expenses for employees (see 5.7).

From 6 April 1983 all private petrol provided by whatever means for directors and higher-paid employees is subject to tax on the scale charge. For non-higher-paid employees private petrol remains tax-free if provided through a company account with a garage or by a company pump.

7.5   Collecting the tax

The amount of the benefit, when determined from the relevant tables and taking account of any allowable contributions, is deducted from the individual's coding allowance so that the tax is collected as part of the normal deductions under the PAYE system.

7.6 Employee-owned cars

Employees who use their own cars for business purposes and meet their own running costs are normally reimbursed by their employers at a certain amount per mile. Such payments are not normally taxable but if, in a particular case, the overall effect is evidently excessive, the Inland Revenue may insist on modifying a flat rate to a tapering rate. Payments made in respect of directors or higher-paid employees (5.3) should be shown on form P11D but a dispensation may be granted (5.7).

Employees who are not classed as higher-paid would not normally be taxable provided that any payments by the employer are not regarded as the discharge of an employee debt (2.1) and the use of a credit card or voucher is not involved (6.2). However, a recent court case has held that mileage allowance was part of an employee's emoluments and was taxable as such. The employer considered it essential for the efficient conduct of business that the employee should use the car, and paid him a mileage allowance for doing so, but it was not a condition of his employment that he should provide his own car for business use. He was therefore not *necessarily* obliged to incur the expense in the performance of his duties and his claim against the Revenue failed (see 4.3).

It is not yet known if this is to become the general treatment of mileage allowances by the Revenue. If mileage allowances are to be taxed in this way this could have serious repercussions for many employees if they cannot fulfil the 'necessarily obliged' test.

An employee who uses his own car for business purposes may claim a 'writing-down allowance' in respect of the depreciation of the car, in addition to the running costs (e.g. insurance, vehicle excise licence). In the first year the allowance is 25 per cent of the cost of the car, the following year it is 25 per cent of the cost less the allowance already given and the same procedure is followed each year, with an adjustment being made when the car is sold. (If the car costs in excess of £8000 the writing-down allowance is restricted to £2000 each year until the balance brought forward falls below £8000.)

The total allowance is given in respect of the business proportion only and any amount received from the employer (as reimbursement of business expenditure) is deducted. In practice, the allowance from the employer is likely to be sufficient not to warrant a further claim being made.

8 Beneficial Loan Arrangements

8.1 Introduction

Specific legislation was introduced, with effect from 6 April 1978, to tax the benefit arising if loans are provided by an employer to an employee at a nil or low rate of interest. This applies to directors or higher-paid employees *only* and employees earning less than £8500 can take advantage of a beneficial loan arrangement without any tax liability arising, provided certain simple rules are followed. There must be no contractual entitlement to the provision of a loan; once granted it must not be transferable or assignable and it should not be 'exchangeable' for increased emoluments at the employee's option.

8.2 Effect of the legislation

Where a director/employee or his relative is provided with an interest-free (or cheap) loan by reason of his employment, he will be taxed on the amount of interest which would have been payable on the loan at the 'official rate' (which is fixed by the Treasury from time to time and is currently 12 per cent per annum), less any amount actually paid.

For this purpose a 'loan' includes:

(1) the granting of credit facilities by an employer to an executive;
(2) indebtedness arising from the facilitating of credit between an executive and third parties by employer guarantees;
(3) salary 'advances'.

8.3 Exemptions

(1) If the director/employee can show that he derived no benefit from a loan made to a relative, there will be no charge to tax.
(2) If the charge calculated under these rules does not exceed £200 it will be exempted from income tax. There are no provisions for marginal relief.
(3) No interest benefit will be charged under these rules if any interest paid would have qualified for income tax relief in the recipient's hands. Under current legislation, interest paid in respect of any of the following types of loans qualifies for income tax relief (this is only a brief summary and the detailed provisions should be looked at in any particular situation):

    (a) loans used for purchasing or improving an individual's principal private residence subject to an upper limit of £30,000; a loan for a further house for a dependent relative may also qualify subject to the same limit in aggregate;

(b) bridging loans for house purchase, subject normally to a time limit of one year, though this is at present extended to two years;

(c) loans used for purchasing or improving property which is let at a commercial rent for at least twenty-six weeks of the year and, when not being let, is available to be let or undergoing repair;

(d) loans used for acquiring shares in a close company or a share in a partnership or providing loans to either type of entity, provided broadly speaking that the individual takes some part in that business;

(e) loans used for purchasing capital equipment for use in the course of the individual's employment duties.

Where, as a result of aggregation of loans outstanding (see 8.4) only a part of the total notional interest qualifies for exemption, the benefit computed will be correspondingly adjusted.

(4) Where a loan was originally made for a fixed term, and at a fixed rate, and the amount of interest paid in the year in which it was made was not less than interest at the official rate for that year, no charge to tax will arise by reason only of a subsequent increase in the official rate.

(5) Where a loan was originally made before 6 April 1978 for a fixed term and at a fixed rate, no tax will arise if it can be shown that the rate of interest would have

been such as would have applied to a loan made on the same terms between persons not 'connected' with each other.

In broad terms an individual is 'connected' with his spouse or with relatives (including their spouses) of his own and his spouse. ('Relative' means brother, sister, ancestor or lineal descendant.) A partner of a business is connected with the person(s) with whom he is in partnership and with their spouses.

8.4 Computing the chargeable benefit

All loans between the same lender and borrower are aggregated and the 'normal' method of computing the notional interest is used unless the Inland Revenue or the individual elect to use the 'alternative' method.

The *normal* method is to calculate the charge by reference to the average of the loan outstanding at the beginning and end of a tax year and the average 'official rate' through the year; if the loan has not been outstanding for the whole of the tax year, the amount of the loan at the time it is granted or redeemed is used for averaging purposes with the amount outstanding at the end or beginning of the tax year as the case may be.

The *alternative* method calculates the notional charge by applying the 'official rate' of interest to the running balance on the loan account on a daily basis through the tax year.

The calculations can be quite complex and where there are substantial sums involved it is recommended that professional advice should be taken to ensure that the most advantageous basis is adopted

8.5 Loan waivers

If any part of a loan, obtained by reason of the employment of a director or higher-paid employee, is released or written off, that amount will be taxed under Schedule E. This includes loans mentioned in 8.3 (2) and (3). No charge arises if:

(1) the employee can show that he derived no benefit from the waiver of a loan made to a relative; or

(2) the waiver takes effect on or after the death of the director/employee; or

(3) the waiver is effected under 'stop-loss' arrangements (see 9.4.3) relating to share-incentive schemes under arrangements entered into prior to 6 April 1976.

In circumstances where loans waived are taxable as income under Schedule E and under some other legislation, the same amounts may not be taxed again under these rules. However, where loans waived may also become taxable under the rules concerning terminal payments, these rules take precedence over the more favourable rules concerning terminal payments. This point should be carefully considered whenever reviewing the detailed arrangements concerning golden handshakes occasioned by retirement or dismissal (see Chapter 11).

9 Acquisition of Shares by Employees

9.1 Introduction

For many years an employee of a company who received shares as part of his remuneration has been liable to income tax under Schedule E on the *value* of the shares received. In more recent years there has been legislation aimed at taxing, at rates applicable to earned income rather than capital gains, the *profits* arising to employees from option schemes and share-incentive schemes. The detailed provisions are complex and only the basic outlines are discussed here.

Throughout this chapter it is assumed that the acquisition of the option or of the shares has been by reason of holding an office or employment (see 1.4).

9.2 Approved share options: the 1984 scheme

Under legislation introduced in the 1984 Finance Act, a new type of share option scheme may be approved by the Inland Revenue which eliminates the income tax charges that can apply on various occasions in relation to earlier 'unapproved' schemes (see 9.3). The conditions summarised below are likely in practice to be less formidable to comply with than would appear at first sight. As a result of their introduction, many companies and groups will be encouraged to set up schemes within these provisions for directors and employees, providing them with a major incentive to the mutual benefit of both employer and employees.

The principal features of the scheme are these:

(1) any gain arising on the exercise of an option is not subject to tax at that stage;
(2) capital gains tax, not income tax, is payable on the disposal of the shares.

Thus share options may be taken out of the income tax net altogether (except in the circumstances mentioned in 9.2.3 below) and the tax payable on the uplift in value of the shares acquired is reduced from a possible 60 per cent to a maximum of 30 per cent.

9.2.1 Participants and their participation

Participants must be directors or employees of the company; while a director is required to be 'full-time' (which in practice means working for the company for at least 25 hours a week), an employee need only be 'part-time' (which requires no more than 20 hours a week). Furthermore, an individual may continue to exercise his rights after he has ceased to work for the company. If the company is 'close' (i.e. controlled by its directors or by five or fewer shareholders, including 'associated' shareholdings for this purpose) or controlled by a close company, there are rules designed to exclude as eligible a shareholder who has or has had a material interest (broadly one representing more than 10 per cent of the share capital) in either the grantor company or the company which controls it.

There is a limit on the value (calculated at the time that the option is granted) of the shares which may be acquired in this way. This is fixed as the greater of:

(a) £100,000; and
(b) four times the individual's earnings in the current or previous year from the employment concerned which are liable to be taxed under PAYE

9.2.2 *Scheme shares*

Shares which may be subject to offer under option in this way must comply with all the following requirements:

(1) they must form part of the company's ordinary share capital;
(2) they must be fully paid up;
(3) they must not be redeemable;
(4) they must not be subject to any restrictions which do not attach to all shares of the same class;
(5) they must be either

    (i) shares of a class quoted on a recognised stock exchange; or

(ii) shares of a company which is not under the control of another company; or

(iii) shares of a company which is under the control of another company whose shares are quoted on a recognised stock exchange (unless the latter company is either a close company or a non-resident one which would be close if it were resident in the UK).

There are special rules where the company has more than one class of share capital.

The company may set up a scheme in respect of

(a) its own shares; or

(b) shares of the company which controls it; or

(c) shares of a company which is, or which has control of, a member of a 'consortium' of companies which either owns the grantor company or the company which controls it. The consortium member must own at least 15 per cent of the ordinary share capital of the company concerned.

It is possible to set up a scheme for a group of companies.

9.2.3   *Grant, exercise and transfer of options*

The price at which scheme shares may be acquired must be stated at the time that the option is granted. It must not be 'manifestly' less than their market value at that time (this is normally taken as not less than 90 per cent of the market value).

If the aggregate of the amount which the individual pays for the option itself and the price at which he may acquire the shares on its exercise is less than the market value of those shares, calculated at the time of the grant of the option, the individual is assessable at that time to income tax on the difference as if it were earned income.

There are certain restrictions imposed on how a participant may deal subsequently with an option which he has been granted, as follows:

(1) he may not transfer it;
(2) he may not exercise it earlier than three years nor later than ten years after the date of the grant;
(3) he may not exercise it within three years of the exercise of a previous option under the same scheme.

Special provisions apply in the event of a participant's death.

9.3 Unapproved share options

A number of arrangements are in operation based on legislation originally introduced in 1972 and subsequently amended; these are generally referred to as 'unapproved schemes'.

In such a scheme there can be up to four occasions when tax may be charged:

(1) *Grant of option*
   A charge to tax is *not* made on the receipt of the option to purchase shares, unless it is capable of being exercised later than seven years after the date it is granted;

78

in that case a charge to tax arises in the tax year in which the option is granted. The charge to tax will be on the excess of the market value of shares at the date of grant over the option price plus the cost of the option itself. A similar charge to tax will arise should the option be released or assigned.

) *Exercise of option*
Where an employee derives a gain by exercising his rights under a share option, and the market value exceeds the option value (plus the cost of the option), a liability to tax arises on the excess in the tax year in which the option is exercised.

As regards any option granted on or before 5 April 1984 which is exercised at any time after 5 April 1983, the tax due may be paid in five equal instalments. The first instalment is due and payable fourteen days after the date that the Collector of Taxes applies for the tax; the last instalment is due on the last day of the fifth tax year following the end of the tax year in which the option is exercised; the second, third and fourth instalments are due at equal intervals between the first and fifth instalments.

This arrangement is applicable where the option is one which is exercisable within seven years of its grant and the price paid for the shares under the terms of the option must not be less than the market value of the relevant shares at the time that the option was granted. In any case, the tax due (taken as arising on the highest slice of the taxpayer's income) must be more than £250; the taxpayer must elect for the instalment arrangement to apply, by notice in writing to the Inspector of Taxes before 4 June following the end of the tax year in which the option is exercised, irrespective of whether an assessment on the gain has been raised.

This instalment facility previously ran over three years, but was extended to five years in the 1984 Finance Act. Where an election for the three-year instalment facility had already been made in relation to an option exercised in the year ended 5 April 1984 (which had to have been made by 4 June 1984), this is automatically extended to five years.

The instalment facility is not available in respect of options *granted* after 5 April 1984.

(3) *Appreciation in value*
Having acquired the shares, another charge to tax will arise on the appreciation in value from the date of acquisition to the earliest of:

(a) the seventh anniversary from the date the option was exercised, and
(b) the date of sale of the shares, and
(c) the removal of any special restrictions attaching to the shares.

This is dealt with in more detail in 9.5.2 below.

(4) *Sale of shares after an earlier charge*
Any appreciation in value on the sale of the shares arising in a period after an earlier charge under (3) above, is taxable according to the normal rules for capital gains tax.

9.4 Savings-related share option schemes

If a company establishes a savings-related share option scheme and it is approved by the Inland Revenue, neither the acquisition of the right, nor its exercise, will give rise to any income tax liability. To obtain approval the scheme must comply with various detailed regulations. Below are listed the main requirements for a scheme to be approved:

(1) The scheme must provide for directors and employees to acquire shares which are part of the ordinary share capital of the company concerned, or of a company which controls it (there are special rules for consortium-owned companies). The shares must be either quoted on the stock exchange, or not be shared in a company controlled by another, or be shares in a subsidiary of a quoted non-close company. They must be fully paid up, not redeemable and not subject to any restrictions other than those which attach to all shares of the same class. If the company has more than one class of shares, the shares to be acquired from the scheme should not be shares of a class the majority of which are held by persons who acquired them by virtue of rights as employees or directors.

(2) The scheme must provide for the shares to be paid for out of repayments made to the employee or director under an approved certified contractual savings scheme (i.e. SAYE). The regular savings must not exceed £50 per month (this limit was increased to £100 per month with effect from 1 September 1984).

(3) Rights obtained under the scheme must not be exercisable before the date (the bonus date) on which repayments under the SAYE scheme become due. (There are exceptions to this.)

(4) The scheme may provide for repayments to be taken as including a bonus or as not including a bonus.

(5) The price at which scheme shares may be acquired must not be 'manifestly less' than 90 per cent of the market value at the time the right is obtained, and must be stated at that time.

(6) The scheme must be open to all those who are employees and directors throughout a qualifying period of not more than five years. They must be resident and ordinarily resident in the UK and liable to tax under Schedule E.

(7) Certain individuals must not be allowed to participate (e.g. if rights have been obtained under another approved scheme established by the company). Otherwise, the scheme must not contain any features which could discourage employees from actually participating and the benefits must not be conferred wholly or mainly on directors or executives of group companies.

Subject to certain conditions, the arrangements are extended to include individuals who have participated in earlier SAYE schemes, including Building Society SAYE contracts. The total monthly contributions, whether under existing schemes or new schemes, must not exceed £50 (now increased to £100 as in (2) above) for the purpose of the tax relief mentioned above.

9.5 Anti-avoidance legislation and pitfalls

Again, the precise provisions are complex and professional advice is strongly recommended before entering into any schemes for employees to acquire shares in employing companies. The main provisions may be considered under three heads.

9.5.1 *Acquisitions at undervalue*

Where an employee derives a benefit by acquiring shares at an undervalue and that benefit is not otherwise chargeable to tax, the benefit arising will be treated as a 'notional loan'. This can have two consequences – first as regards possible tax liability on cheap or interest-free loans (see Chapter 8) and second, as regards the benefits arising on waiver of loans (see 8.5). The notional loan ceases when the amounts outstanding are paid or the shares are sold or the employee dies.

9.5.2 *Non-exempted acquisitions*

Unless the acquisition is exempted under one of the conditions set out below, then regardless of whether the acquisition was a straightforward purchase or on the exercise of an option or otherwise, the appreciation in value from the date of acquisition will be subject to income tax on the earliest of the three occasions mentioned in 9.3(3) above.

If, however, one of the exemptions applies, the income tax charge will be replaced by a capital gains tax charge at the date of disposal.

The exact circumstances in which the acquisition will be exempted are complex, and it is safest first to assume that the acquisition will give rise to a subsequent income tax charge and then to see if an available exemption fits the circumstances.

Broadly speaking, the acquisition is exempted under one of the following circumstances:

(1) the shares are acquired in pursuance of an offer to the public; or

(2) the shares are of a class of which the majority are acquired by non-directors and non-employees (but excluding those held through an associated company). The exemption does not apply if any of the following special restrictions attach to the shares or the holding of the shares:

(a) restrictions not attaching to *all* shares of that same class;

(b) restrictions which may be lifted at some future time;

(c) restrictions applying to the shares so long as they are held by directors or employees (except a stipulation for the sale thereof to a specified person at a price not exceeding market value on leaving employment);

(d) restrictions on the shares through being used as a security for any loan made or facilitated by the employer (or an associated company or certain shareholders) unless so done in the ordinary course of the business of making personal loans; or

84

(3) the shares are acquired by directors and employees who through those shares (excluding any shares held through an associated company) can control the employing company. There must be no special restrictions of the sort outlined under (a), (b) or (d) of (2) above; or

(4) the shares are acquired under a 'profit-sharing scheme' (see 9.7).

9.5.3 *'Stop-loss' arrangements*

Many share-option and -incentive schemes contained provisions whereby the employees were protected against a fall in the value of shares acquired. This was effected in a variety of ways such as by the repurchase of shares at their original value, or the satisfaction of unpaid purchase money up to the lower value if the shares had fallen in value. Under specific legislation, such provisions are now treated as conferring an additional taxable benefit on employees in the form of a notional loan waiver as in 9.5.1 above.

9.6 Returns and information

A company is required to provide the following information to the Inspector of Taxes within thirty days of the end of the relevant year of assessment:

(1) the grant, exercise, assignment, transfer, waiver or release of any share options which may give rise to an income tax liability as regards the employees; and

(2) the allotment of any shares under such option or incentive schemes.

9.7   Profit-sharing schemes

Where a director (or employee) acquires shares as part of his emoluments (i.e. he is taxed on their value at the time of acquisition), the appreciation in value may be subject only to capital gains tax provided the scheme meets all the following conditions:

(1) the shares in question must be those of the employing company (or those of a company which controls that employing company);
(2) the entitlement to shares must be dependent on the level of profits of the company and the proportion of profits allocated to the scheme must be determined *in advance*. Normally a fixed percentage for the duration of the scheme is advisable but it may be possible to vary the percentage;
(3) the shares must be quoted on a recognized stock exchange *or* be in a company not controlled by another;
(4) the scheme must be open to all UK-domiciled employees (i.e. persons who think of the UK as their natural homeland, normally those people who were born here) over 25 years of age who are resident and ordinarily resident in this country and who have been in the company's employment for at least five years;
(5) the shares must not be subject to restrictions which are capable of being lifted and as a result of which the value of the shares may rise.

To make profit-sharing schemes more attractive a new scheme was introduced which applies to shares acquired by the employee after 5 April 1979. Under this scheme the initial market value of shares which may be transferred to any employee each year is the greater of £1,250 or 10 per cent of the employee's earnings, subject to an annual limit of £5,000. (In this case, 'earnings' normally means pay as taken for PAYE purposes.) The shares have to be held by trustees for the employees until disposed of or released (once the seven-year period has passed) but the employee will receive any dividend payments which are made. The shareholding must be retained for at least two years except for occasions of attaining retirement age, cessation of employment of the employee concerned, or death.

No income tax liability will arise on the original value of the appropriated shares if the release date is seven years from the date of acquisition (or, if earlier, the death of the employee). If there is a disposal of scheme shares before the release date, income tax will be payable on a proportion of the original market value of the shares (or, if less, the disposal proceeds) as follows:

Up to 4 years	100%
4–5 years	75%
5–6 years	50%
6–7 years	25%

If the employee ceases his employment or reaches retirement age the proportion is 50 per cent for the first six years and 25 per cent in the seventh year.

10 Pensions for the Employed

10.1 The role of the State

The basic element in almost everyone's retirement income is the flat-rate State retirement pension. This is payable if full national insurance contributions have been paid for at least nine-tenths of the individual's working life. A woman entitled to a pension in her own right will normally receive it at the age of 60, a man at the age of 65. A married man will receive an additional amount for his wife but if she is entitled to pensions in respect of both her own and her husband's contributions, she may claim whichever is the higher pension.

In addition to paying national insurance contributions it is advisable also to pay into a pension scheme. It is the role of the State to make sure that schemes run privately by employers meet certain standards and in cases where the pensions granted by such schemes have their value eroded by inflation, the State supplements the pension payable (see 10.5).

There is a national earnings-related pension scheme run by the State, and since 1978 every employer has had to pay into the State scheme for all his employees unless he is running an approved private scheme.

For the position of British nationals working overseas see 12.15.

10.2   The State scheme

The State scheme offers a considerable improvement on the terms of pension schemes that were being run before 1978. All the benefits increase in line with the increases in the retail prices index, but there are still a number of disadvantages that the State scheme has when compared with a private occupational scheme that has been duly approved. There can be no flexibility on the age of retirement. There is no income tax relief for the individual's payments into the scheme, and at the present time (1984/85) earnings over £13,000 are unpensionable.

For the purposes of the State scheme an employee's pay is divided into three bands. The first is that part of his pay up to the level of the basic retirement pension at the beginning of the tax year. This is the part on which everyone pays contributions and goes towards building up the pension entitlement (see 10.1).

The second band falls between the basic pension rate and about seven times that amount. In a great number of cases this covers all the pay of an employee. For anyone paying into the State scheme the second band earnings are his pensionable pay – the earnings-related pension he will eventually receive will be calculated on them.

The third band is pay any employee receives over the

upper limit of the second band (for 1984/85, £13,000). This is the part on which no pension can be provided through the State scheme.

For anyone who has been in the scheme more than twenty years his pension will be the total of his best twenty years' revalued entitlements. In the case of individuals with twenty or fewer years of contributions, all their entitlements will be counted. Before retirement, the revaluation of pension entitlements will be based on increases in national pay averages. Afterwards, pension values will rise in line with the retail prices index.

The disadvantages of the State scheme have been pointed out above. To a large extent these problems can be overcome even when there is no private scheme available – see top-hat schemes (10.11) and personal pension plans (10.13).

10.3 Private schemes – requirements for approval

An employer may run his occupational pension scheme either 'in-house' or through a life assurance company. Irrespective of who is running the scheme, it *must* be approved by the Inland Revenue Superannuation Funds Office and by the Occupational Pensions Board, if he is to be allowed to 'contract out' of the State scheme.

Members who are contracted out of the State scheme will still be entitled to the State flat-rate benefits, but not to the earnings-related element.

The benefits the scheme offers must, at least, be as good as those provided by the State scheme. The main requirements may be summarised as follows:

(1) arrangements must be under an irrevocable trust;
(2) maximum pension should not exceed two-thirds of the 'final salary' (see 10.3.1) for a minimum of ten years' service and should be reduced where a lump-sum payment is made at the date of retirement;
(3) maximum lump-sum payment (tax-free) of 1.5 times 'final salary' (see 10.3.1) may be payable for a minimum of twenty years' service and part-commutation of pension entitlements;
(4) maximum pension payable to widow on member's death in retirement should not exceed two-thirds of the member's own pension entitlement;
(5) maximum lump sum (free of income tax) on death in service, amounting to four times the then salary, may be paid to dependents and will be free of capital transfer tax if the payment is at the employer's discretion. The scheme rules may also provide for the return of contributions made;
(6) on death in service, widow's pension should not exceed two-thirds of the pension the member could have received had he retired on incapacity grounds at the date of his death;
(7) benefits may be increased after retirement, up to certain limits either by meeting the cost out of the fund's surpluses, or by special contributions by the employer (see 10.5).

10.3.1 Definition of 'final salary'

This is defined as either:

(1) any of the previous five years' emoluments, or

(2) the average of the best three or more consecutive years' emoluments ending no more than ten years prior to retirement. This definition is obligatory for '20 per cent directors', i.e. those who control directly or indirectly more than 20 per cent of the voting shares.

'Controlling' directors (i.e. those with 5 per cent or more of the share capital) may participate in occupational pension schemes of their companies.

As the contracting-in or -out rules did not take effect until 1978, employers are not required to give credit for service before that date. In practice, however, most contracted-out employers had occupational schemes before 1978 and so will pay pensions in respect of service before these rules came into effect.

Partly due to the complexity of the legislation and partly due to the fact that the requirements of various employees and employers are so different, each scheme is essentially tailor-made to suit particular needs. In practice, this entails liaison between the company, representatives of the employees, accountants, solicitors and insurance brokers in devising a suitable scheme.

10.4   Approval refused – the consequences

Although this is unlikely to happen in practice, if a scheme is not approved by the Inland Revenue there could be any or all of the following consequences:

(1) disallowance of members' contributions for income tax purposes;

(2) disallowance of employer's contributions for corporation tax purposes;
(3) full taxation of all income and capital gains of the fund (approved funds are exempt from income tax and capital gains tax);
(4) income tax liability on employee for employer's contributions to scheme on his behalf;
(5) unfavourable treatment of benefits.

Under certain circumstances the Board of Inland Revenue has discretion to approve an occupational pension scheme for tax purposes even though it does not fully satisfy the strict conditions for approval laid down in the legislation.

10.5   Guaranteed minimum pensions

Employers are not obliged to increase pensions once they are in payment. This is why the State provides supplementary bonuses partially to protect contracted-out pensions from inflation (see 10.1). The State bonuses are linked to that part of a person's pension which he would have received if he had been in the State earnings-related scheme instead. This is called the 'guaranteed minimum pension'. The State inflation-proofing is provided in addition to any increase paid by the employer. Some employers provide almost full inflation-proofing for the employees' pensions; others provide occasional rises which only partly compensate for inflation.

10.6   Pension rights when changing jobs

An employee who moves from one contracted-out employer to another may lose part of his pension rights. He may have a choice of:

(1) accepting a frozen pension (see below), or
(2) transferring his pension rights to his new employer, or
(3) extinguishing part of his pension rights in return for a refund of some contributions. Refunds will usually be available only for contributions made before April 1975 or for short periods of service.

A 'frozen' pension is a pension preserved by the former employer and normally linked to the employee's pay at the date the employment ceased. In its basic form this provides no protection against inflation. If pay levels rise before retirement a pension linked to a salary from years ago will look very small when it is paid. Due to the State earnings-related provisions, at least part of an employee's entitlement is inflation-proofed under the guaranteed minimum pension arrangements for contracted-out schemes (see 10.5).

In some cases the burden of preserving the guaranteed minimum pension entitlement may be transferred to the new employer. In view of the inflation-proofing required few employers are prepared to take this on.

The remainder of a contracted-out employee's pension rights (i.e. the part not covered by the guaranteed minimum pension provisions) will normally remain with his former employer to be paid when he eventually retires. The old employer can, in theory, transfer the bill to the new employer but this is a rare occurrence.

Increasing concern has been shown recently at the erosion of an individual's pension entitlement that may follow from a change of job, and the Department of Health and Social Security are examining ways in which better arrangements for the 'portability' of occupational pension rights may be set up.

10.7 Termination of employment – contributions made

Where, as part of a termination agreement, the employer makes a special contribution to an approved scheme to provide benefits for the employee, the Revenue have stated that they will not seek to charge such a payment under the provisions taxing lump-sum payments. This is provided that the benefits on retirement are within the limits and in the form prescribed by the rules of the scheme.

The subject of termination payments is dealt with in Chapter 11.

10.8 Self-administered pension schemes

Considerable interest has been shown in recent years in the development of the so-called 'self-administered' pension schemes, particularly where only a small number of individuals is to be covered.

The essence of such a scheme is to remove the operation of the fund from the hands of a life assurance company or a body of independent trustees and to give control over the fund's assets and investment decisions to the members themselves. In particular the fund may then be able to invest the contributions it receives back in the company itself, either by loans or by subscription for shares or perhaps by purchasing and leasing back certain assets, such as property, from the company. It should be noted however that the Superannuation Funds Office will normally only allow 'inside' investment of this kind up to a maximum of 50 per cent of the fund's assets.

In addition, the Superannuation Funds Office, before giving approval to the fund, will require the appointment of a 'pensioneer trustee' as one of the trustees of the fund. This has to be an individual or a body, independent of the company, who is well experienced in the field of occupational pension schemes; on appointment he is required to give certain undertakings as to the winding-up of the scheme and as to its management generally.

While the concept has many attractions, particularly on the investment side, it does need to be considered with care, particularly to ensure that the interests of all members are adequately protected. It is essential that specialist professional advice, in the legal and taxation field as well as in the pension area itself, be obtained before going into such a scheme.

10.9 Sick-pay and disability schemes

Where an employee receives any sums which are paid in connection with his absence from work through sickness or disability, as a result of arrangements entered into by his employer, then the sums will be taxed under Schedule E. Sums paid to a member of the employee's 'family or household' (i.e. spouse, sons and daughters and their spouses, his parents and his dependants) or to the order or benefit of the employee or his household are to be similarly taxed.

Where the scheme is funded by contributions from both employer and employee, only that part of the sick pay attributable to the employer's contributions will be taxable.

These provisions were introduced by the Finance Act 1981 and applied from 1983/84 where the sick pay was paid under a scheme already in force on 4 June 1981 and from 1982/83 in other cases.

The right of a higher-paid employee or director to receive such sums is not to be classed as a taxable benefit, i.e. the cost to the employer of providing such sick-pay cover will not of itself be taxed as a benefit in kind.

These provisions have been enacted to counter schemes under which sick pay, provided at the employer's expense under an insurance policy or trust deed, has been paid directly by the insurance company, thereby avoiding the need for the employer to account for PAYE or national insurance contributions. The schemes also took advantage of a Revenue concession which granted a tax holiday of up to two years on sickness benefits paid under insurance policies. This concession will be amended to exclude employer-financed sickness-pay schemes and the employer-financed proportion of jointly funded schemes. The concession will continue to apply to benefits paid under schemes entered into and financed by individuals, or to the employee's proportion where the scheme is funded jointly.

It should also be noted that payments under the 'statutory sick pay' scheme which came into operation on 6 April 1983 are liable to PAYE and national insurance contributions.

10.10   Death-in-service and accident policies

An occupational pension scheme may provide for injury cover such as lump-sum payments on loss of limbs and/or life cover. In such circumstances, it is normal practice for the Inland Revenue to ignore the taxable benefit arising in respect of a proportion of the contributions and in any case the point is normally settled at the time of negotiation in seeking 'approval' of the scheme. In such cases, it is most important to demonstrate that the benefits arising are 'discretionary' and consequently it is necessary to ensure that the employer first becomes entitled to the benefits under the scheme (the subsequent payment to the employee or his dependents being a separate transaction). If injury and life cover are provided under a separate scheme, any taxable benefit that may arise will be valued under the general rules (see 5.5 and 5.6).

Alternatively, an employer may make *voluntary* payments on death or in the event of injury. If a lump sum is paid it will be tax-free, but if a series of recurring payments (i.e. a 'discretionary' pension) is involved, they may be taxed as earned income. The capital sum may be used for purchasing an annuity and the capital element thereof will be free of income tax. A difficult consideration is the question of the deductibility of the payments as regards the employer, and particularly so if the recipient has a significant share ownership in the company. If the payments are disallowed and the employer company is close, there may be capital transfer tax consequences as well. Broadly speaking, a close company is a company that is controlled by five or fewer of its shareholders, or by its directors.

10.11 'Top-hat' and 'key-man' schemes

It will be seen from 10.2 above that employees who are contracted in may have unpensionable earnings. If this is so, it is possible for the individual employee to make his own pension arrangements with an insurance company in respect of the unpensioned salary. It is also possible to build into such schemes benefits missing from the State scheme, e.g. tax-free lump sums on retirement or death in service. If the employer pays the contribution it is not classed as a benefit. Tax relief is available on the employee's contributions provided they do not exceed 15 per cent of the earnings. These schemes are referred to as 'top-hat' policies.

In addition to this it is also possible to set up a small self-administered scheme (see 10.9) for one person or a small group of people who hold key positions in a business, hence the title 'key-man'. This can incorporate 'loanback' facilities for the director or employee concerned.

Loanback facilities are available from a number of insurance companies which enable the person taking out the policy to borrow back the larger part, if not all, of the capital invested, paying interest at a commercial rate.

10.12 Additional voluntary contributions

An individual may set aside up to 15 per cent of his remuneration by way of contributions to an approved pension fund of which he is a member. In practice the contributions required from members in accordance with scheme rules are less, and sometimes substantially less, than this. In principle it is open to an employee to boost his eventual benefits by making further contributions (know as 'additional voluntary contributions' or 'AVCs') up to the 15 per cent limit.

There are two practical requirements that have to be met before this facility can be made use of:

(1) the scheme itself must contain explicit provision to accept AVCs (in practice, most schemes do);
(2) contributions have to be made on a regular basis and the Superannuation Funds Office normally require this to be done over at least five years. (They will probably not insist on this where the individual is just approaching retirement age or where he is made redundant and cannot keep the payments up.)

Although the benefits attributable to AVCs are paid out through the pension scheme when they mature, they are kept separate from the rest of the fund. Thus they cannot be used to make up any deficiencies arising elsewhere in the fund and the employee may take the contributions, inviolate, with him if he changes jobs. It may also be possible for the individual, in conjunction with the pension fund manager, to have some involvement in how his contributions may be invested; in some cases, this may even be arranged in a separate managed fund for each contributor.

10.13   Personal pension plans

Individuals in non-pensionable employments who make their own retirement arrangements by payment of premiums out of their earnings are entitled to tax relief on contributions made, in the same way as self-employed individuals (i.e. a self-employed retirement annuity policy). To qualify for tax relief the premiums payable should be in respect of an 'approved' scheme and an insurance company will normally obtain Inland Revenue 'approval' for its retirement pension scheme. As compared to benefits under a conventional pension scheme, the benefits of a retirement annuity policy are less favourable and, in practice, only those who are not able to participate in a pension scheme (principally the self-employed) consider taking out a retirement annuity contract.

For many individuals, a very important consideration is that an employer often makes substantial contributions to a pension scheme on an individual's behalf whereas contributions under a retirement annuity contract are entirely out of an individual's own resources. In addition, quite apart from other considerations, benefits payable under a pension scheme are enhanced because of the number of participants. In contrast, retirement annuity contracts are normally on an individual basis.

Premiums paid under retirement annuity contracts qualify for a deduction from the individual's non-pensionable earnings. The maximum amount that may be claimed as a deduction varies as a percentage of the individual's *net relevant earnings*, depending on his age, as follows:

Year of birth	Percentage of net relevant earnings
1934 or later	17.5
1916 to 1933	20
1914 or 1915	21
1912 or 1913	24
1910 or 1911	26.5
1908 or 1909	29.5
1907	32.5

Out of the above percentages, premiums not exceeding 5 per cent of the net relevant earnings may be used to take out term life assurance for the benefit of the individual's wife or husband or other dependants, in effect to provide a form of death-in-service benefit. This arrangement cannot be used to fund an endowment or whole-life assurance policy.

The term 'net relevant earnings' means the earnings from the individual's self-employment (or a non-pensionable employment) having taken into account losses, stock relief and capital allowances. The relief will normally be given against income of the tax year in which the premium is paid but an election can be made which allows a premium to be treated as paid in the previous tax year, or, if there were no relevant earnings in that year, in the tax year before that.

Where the maximum amount of relief which would be available exceeds the premiums paid in a year, the excess (known as *unused relief*) may be carried forward for up to six years and used when the reverse situation arises and the premiums paid exceed the amount allowable. Relief claimed in this way must be used in the earliest possible year. The relief, introduced in 1980, may be backdated for six years, but is forfeited once the six-year period comes to an end unless the provisions for 'relating back' described in the previous paragraph are used.

Thus unused relief for 1977/78 would normally be lost by 5 April 1984. However, a premium paid in 1984/85 could be related back and treated as if it had been paid in 1983/84. If this gave rise to excess premiums in 1983/84 this excess could be absorbed by the unused relief from 1977/78.

10.13.1 *Capital commutation and transfer*

Although the primary purpose of a personal pension plan as described in 10.12 is the provision of a pension on retirement (which must normally take place between 60 and 75, although an earlier retirement age can be negotiated in special cases), it is open to the individual to commute a part of the pension for a tax-free capital sum at the time of his retirement. The maximum amount that may be commuted in this way is three times the annual amount of the annuity remaining.

It is also open to the individual, at the time of his retirement, to have the benefits of any existing personal pension plan transferred to another company, if he considers that this will give him a better deal.

10.13.2   *Loanback arrangements*

Similar to the 'inside' investment idea which can be used in conjunction with a self-administered pension scheme (see 10.8), it may also be possible to obtain loanback facilities in connection with a personal pension plan. These generally follow one of these forms:

(1) The individual borrows from the insurance company concerned an amount up to the total level of the contributions that he has paid in, on which loan he pays interest. This interest is credited specifically to the fund represented by the loan, after a deduction for expenses; it may be deductible for tax purposes to the payer if the loan is used for a 'qualifying purpose'.

The loan will normally be repaid out of the cash commutation that may be taken when the policy matures, but conditions as to early repayment may be imposed if contributions are to be reduced or cease. In the meantime, the insurance company will normally require some suitable security for the loan.

(2) Larger sums, up to possibly ten times the individual's annual contributions or 2.5 times his annual income,

may be borrowed on security at a commercial rate of interest from the insurance company. The rate of interest will normally be fixed at the time that the loan is taken out (which may make the proposition less attractive at a time of falling interest rates). Again, re-payment will normally come out of the cash commutation, with early repayment only arising on default or failure of security.

As well as the purely commercial aspects of such schemes, consideration may need also to be given to the following:

(1) the long-term wisdom of an individual investing his future pension in a loan to himself with no capital growth, however vital the short-term need;
(2) the possibility that the Revenue may not take kindly to funds going back into the contributor's pocket, perhaps at a subsidy from themselves, bearing in mind that self-administered employee pension schemes are only allowed at best a 50 per cent loanback facility.

11 Termination Payments

11.1 Introduction

The fact that there is an exemption from tax for termination payments is widely known. However, the detailed rules were substantially modified by the 1981 Finance Act and further changes were made as regards payments made after 5 April 1982 by the 1982 Finance Act.

An appropriate place to begin is to consider circumstances where no exemption is available. The definition of 'emoluments' (see 2.1) excludes a 'capital' sum as income tax is a tax on income. However, the Inland Revenue have successfully argued in the courts that a payment is not 'capital' merely because it is relatively large. The decision is essentially a question of fact (see 11.2).

If the payments are in fact 'emoluments', income tax liability will arise in full with no special relief. If the payments are *not* 'emoluments', they would have been tax-free had it not been for specific legislation which prescribes how such sums are to be taxed. Even then three basic considerations arise:

(1) certain payments may be exempt from tax altogether (see 11.3);

(2) the first part of the lump sums may be exempt (see 11.4);
(3) after taking into account (1) and (2) above the remainder of the sums received may be taxed at a reduced rate (see 11.6).

The above basic principles apply to the taxation of a majority of the lump-sum payments commonly encountered in practice such as ex-gratia payments, payments for commuting pension rights, redundancy payments and compensation for unfair dismissal or for loss of office. Special considerations apply to the following:

(1) payments for restrictive covenants (see 11.8);
(2) payments for variation of service agreements (see 11.9);
(3) payments for inducing an individual to give up employment (see 11.10).

Unless otherwise stated, what follows applies to *all* employees and directors.

Long-service awards are dealt with at 2.3.

11.2 Capital or income

Since this is a question of fact, each situation has to be considered on its merits and over the years there have been a number of cases on this point. The following guidelines should be followed, but, as with many areas of tax legislation, the list is not exhaustive and no one factor or piece of evidence may be regarded as conclusive:

(1) A payment in accordance with a contractual commitment (e.g. as specified in the individual's employment contract or, as in the case of directors of family companies, as specified in the company's articles of association) will almost certainly be taxable as an emolument.

(2) A payment in recognition of past services will be taxed in full as additional remuneration for those services. Care is clearly necessary in the documentation relating to any termination payment to ensure that the Revenue cannot contend that it falls into this category. No formal decision to make any ex-gratia payment should be recorded as being taken until after the employee has left the employer's service.

(3) Similarly a payment associated with any commitment by an individual as to his future role or relationship with the employer may be regarded as advance remuneration (i.e. in respect of services to be performed in the future). Consequently, it is better to pay a lump sum on or after termination of employment unconditionally rather than to pay the same sum on an understanding such as that the employee will assist his successor from time to time after his employment has ceased. Likewise care is necessary if the employee is to be paid a lump sum (on retirement or resignation from the employment) and is subsequently engaged as a 'consultant' or in some other capacity.

(4) As evidence of the precise terms of understanding and

the nature of payments, the Inland Revenue may require to see all documentation and it is as well therefore for draft documents to be scrutinised and settled beforehand. This is of application to such documents as board minutes, internal memoranda, letters exchanged between the parties and so forth.

11.3   Exempt lump sums

The following lump sums are exempt from tax altogether:

(1) death benefits and sums in respect of injury or disability (see below);
(2) lump sums from approved pension schemes for part-commutation of pensions (see 10.3(3) and 10.13.1);
(3) lump sums in respect of an office or employment in which the individual's duties included specified periods of foreign service. There was also a special 50 per cent exemption where an individual not domiciled in the UK received a lump-sum payment from his non-resident employer before 1 August 1984, in respect of a termination which occurred before 12 March 1984.

With regard to (1) above the Revenue have stated that 'disability' covers not only a condition resulting from a sudden affliction but also continuing incapacity to perform the duties of an office or employment arising out of the culmination of a process of deterioriation of physical or mental health caused by chronic illness.

11.4   Tax-free part of a lump sum

In what follows, it should be noted that it is the date of termination, i.e. when the office or employment comes to an end, that is relevant, not the date of payment.

Lump-sum payments which are not taxable in full as 'emoluments' on termination of employment are exempt to the extent of the first £25,000. This exemption is in addition to the sums exempted in 11.3. (Prior to 6 April 1981 the limit was £10,000 though this might be greater for ex-gratia payments under certain circumstances.)

This does not apply to payments for restrictive covenants (11.8), variation of service agreements (11.9) and inducing an individual to give up employment (11.10).

11.5   The old and the new – which rules apply

The current rules apply to lump sums in respect of terminations taking place after 6 April 1981. Where a payment is received in respect of such a termination occurring after that date, but arrangements were entered into before 10 March 1981, the individual may elect to be taxed under the previous rules if this is to his advantage. The election must be made within six years.

The previous rules continue to apply to terminations occurring up to and including 5 April 1981.

There may be cases where the new exemption of £25,000 is to be set against a number of associated payments, one or more of which was received before 6 April 1981, and one or more of which was received after that date. If this is so, only £10,000 of the total exemption is to be deducted from the payments received before 6 April 1981.

11.6   The charge to tax

For a termination taking place on or before 5 April 1981 the computations were complex and are not dealt with here.

For a termination taking place between 6 April 1981 and 5 April 1982, both dates inclusive, the income tax payable was one-half of the additional tax that would have been payable if the excess of the lump sum over £25,000 had been taxed as income.

For a termination taking place on or after 6 April 1982, this 'top-slicing' relief has been modified, so that tax on the excess of the lump sum over £25,000 is now relieved as follows:

next £25,000   –   tax reduced by a half
next £25,000   –   tax reduced by a quarter
excess over £75,000 –   no reduction in tax

Example 8
Mr T. Rend has his employment terminated in 1984/85 and receives a lump-sum payment of £90,000. His income and allowances are as follows:

	£	£
Earnings from employment	45,000	
Other income	2,000	
Lump-sum termination payment	90,000	
Personal allowance	3,155	

Liability excluding lump sum:

	£	
Earnings	45,000	
Other income	2,000	
	47,000	
Personal allowance	3,155	
Taxable income	£43,845	
Tax liability		£19,267
(taxpayer's top rate is 60%)		

Liability on lump sum:

	£	
Lump sum	90,000	
Exempt	25,000	
	£65,000	
Tax on £25,000 at 60%	15,000	
Reduced by a half	7,500	7,500
Tax on £25,000 at 60%	15,000	
Reduced by a quarter	3,750	11,250
Tax on balance of £15,000 at 60%		9,000
Tax liability		£27,750
Total tax liability		£47,017

11.7 Redundancy payments

Statutory redundancy payments are exempt from income tax under Schedule E with the exception of any liability under the provisions taxing lump sum payments.

Non-statutory redundancy payments may be taxable in full if the payments are a condition of the employment or the employees expect such payments.

The Revenue have clarified the conditions under which the £25,000 exemption and the top-slicing relief will be given against non-statutory redundancy payments:

(1) the redundancy must be genuine;
(2) the employee must have been continuously in the service of the employer for at least two years;
(3) the payments are not made to selected employees only;
(4) the payments are not excessive in relation to earnings and length of service.

If an employer proposes to make such payments without deducting tax the arrangements should be cleared, in advance, with the Inspector of Taxes (see also 10.7 and 11.11).

11.8 Restrictive covenants

There are special provisions concerning the taxation of a payment by an employer to an employee in return for the employee undertaking to restrict his own business activities in direct competition with the business of the employer. It is not essential that such a payment is made on the termination of an employment, although in practice this is more common than for a payment to be made at the commencement of, or during the currency of, the employment.

A payment in respect of restrictive covenants is normally regarded as being expenditure on enhancing goodwill and so far as the payer is concerned will only qualify against capital gains on the sale of the business.

As regards the recipient, the tax liability is computed by 'grossing up' the sum received at the basic rate of tax and assessing higher-rate tax only on the grossed sum (i.e. giving credit for the notional basic-rate tax included in the grossing up).

Other points to note in considering a payment for restrictive covenants are:

(1) In certain circumstances, the Inland Revenue may argue that a payment on termination was for past services or that a payment on commencement was for future services (see 11.2(3)). It is therefore strongly recommended that arrangements for such payments are clearly set out in writing and professional advice should be sought if necessary.

(2) The employer must provide the Inland Revenue with details of such payments by 5 May following the end of the tax year in which the payments are made.

(3) Since such payments are disallowed in computing the employer's liability to tax, any tax planning in this area should carefully consider the position if the same sums had been paid as additional salary.

114

11.9   Variation of service agreements

There are practical difficulties in deciding whether a particular payment is in respect of past or future services (see 11.2), or altogether exempt from tax. Perhaps it is useful to summarise briefly the decisions in two important cases on this subject:

(1) A payment of £40,000 was made to an employee in return for accepting a lower rate of remuneration in future. The duties of the employee remained essentially the same prior and subsequent to that payment and the entire sum fell to be taxed as income in the year of receipt.

(2) An employer company paid £10,000 to an individual in return for his resignation as chairman (he continued to serve as a director) and the payment was held to be capital. Considerable weight was attached to the fact that there *was* an alteration in the nature of duties and that he agreed not to pursue any contingent claim for compensation on relinquishing his chairmanship.

In the right circumstances it would appear to be open to an employer to pay a lump sum to an employee if he were demoted or given a less responsible job, etc. The case would be particularly strong if the employee could have had legal remedies under the employment legislation or perhaps a claim for unfair discrimination. However, the point is by no means clear-cut and professional advice should always be sought.

11.10 Inducing an employee to give up employment

It appears that a payment made by a prospective employer to induce an individual to give up his current occupation is quite distinct from inducements offered to him to take up his new employment. It is a question of fact as to what the payment relates and the Revenue will seek to treat such sums as advance remuneration. The onus of proof as to the precise nature of such a payment is on the employer and employee.

From cases that have been considered by the courts it seems that payments in this category would be either free of all tax or taxable as income, as the specific legislation concerning lump-sum payments and exemptions only applies to *termination* payments as such. It also seems that to succeed in establishing the payment as tax-free, it must not be made by the prospective employer.

Professional advice is strongly recommended before agreeing to make or receive such a payment.

11.11 The employer's position

As with any revenue expenditure borne by an employer, the test for tax relief is whether the expenditure was incurred 'wholly and exclusively' for the purposes of the trade. This requirement is normally considered to be met so far as termination payments are concerned on the grounds that by paying a lump sum the employer is taking a commercial decision in saving legal costs, or disposing of the onerous liability of keeping an employee whose services may not be required, or generally behaving as a 'good employer'. However, the position is materially different if the payment is linked with events such as a liquidation, a transfer or cessation of trade, change of employer ownership on a takeover and so on. In such circumstances, the burden of showing that the expenditure was incurred 'wholly and exclusively' for the purpose of the business and not in connection with the liquidation, etc., is likely to be heavier.

Redundancy costs incurred in accordance with the requirements of current employment legislation are normally allowable deductions for the employer. Redundancy payments made specifically on cessation of a trade or business additional to the statutory amount and up to three times that amount, will normally be allowed as a trading deduction. If payment is made after cessation it will be treated as made on the last day of trading.

It is the responsibility of the employer to deduct PAYE from lump sums paid. To avoid excessive overpayments of tax, the approval of the Inland Revenue should be sought (through professional advisers where necessary) as to the provisional tax liability of the individual concerned. If this is not done the employer is required to deduct tax from the whole of the payment in excess of £25,000. Only basic rate tax should be deducted if the payments are made after the form P45 has been issued. If the Revenue is approached in sufficient time in advance instructions will normally be issued for the PAYE deduction to take account of the various reliefs, at least on a provisional basis.

Finally, employers are also required to provide the

Inland Revenue with details of all taxable lump-sum payments made (including tax deducted at source) by 5 May following the end of the tax year in which they are made.

12 British Nationals Working Overseas

12.1 Introduction

The United Kingdom tax liability of an individual who is normally living in the UK but who has an overseas employment can be affected by three factors; his *domicile*, his *residence status* and whether or not he is *ordinarily resident*. These terms are not defined in the taxing statutes but are based on a substantial body of case law going back over many years and on Inland Revenue practice which has developed over that period.

12.2 Domicile

A person's 'domicile' is essentially the country which he looks on as his natural homeland. It is quite distinct from legal nationality and from residence. A person starts with a 'domicile of origin' which is normally his father's domicile at that time; he retains this until he acquires a 'domicile of choice' which can only be done by severing his ties with the domicile of origin and producing evidence of a firm intention of settling permanently in another country. For example in the case of a US citizen who was born in the United States and whose father was born in the United States also, it would be practically impossible for the UK Inland Revenue to prove that he had a United Kingdom domicile, unless he had shown by the way in which he conducted his life that not only did he no longer regard the US as his natural homeland, but that he had adopted the UK as such in its place.

The tax position of an individual who is resident in the UK but domiciled overseas is looked at in Chapter 13.

12.3   Residence and ordinary residence

For tax purposes, residence and ordinary residence normally have to be decided for a tax year. An individual who has been habitually resident in the UK will be regarded as resident in this country if any absence abroad is purely temporary. 'Temporary' is defined as 'occasional'. This statutory definition would have made it difficult for a British subject to shed his 'residence' had it not been for a well-established Inland Revenue concession which is discussed below.

'Ordinarily resident' means habitually resident. A person could in theory be ordinarily resident for a tax year for which he was absent from the UK for the whole year and therefore not resident – if, for example, he goes to Tahiti for a holiday and stays for a whole tax year. Similarly, it is possible for an individual to be resident but not ordinarily resident – for example if he normally lives overseas but happens to spend more than 183 days in the UK in a particular tax year (or even sets foot here at all, if he has a place of abode available for his use and an employment is not involved. See 12.3.2.). Neither of these situations is likely to arise in the instance of a UK national taking up overseas employment, and for most purposes the distinction between residence and ordinary residence need not concern such an individual.

However, in the opposite circumstances, for an individual domiciled abroad coming to the UK for employment and intending to remain for two years or more, he will be regarded as being here for other than a temporary purpose and in practice would be treated as being resident from the date of his arrival. Apart from this, if an individual comes to the UK intending at the outset to remain for three years or more he would, in accordance with normal Revenue practice, be regarded as resident and ordinarily resident from the date of arrival.

It is possible to be resident for tax purposes in more than one country, and a person cannot claim that he is not resident in the UK merely because he is resident somewhere else. However, some double tax treaties provide that a person can only be a resident of one of the countries concerned for purposes of the agreement, and the concept of residence is more narrowly defined in such agreements so as to avoid ambiguity.

Legally, a person is either resident or not resident for a *whole* tax year, but by concession tax years may be split for this purpose. In particular, if a person goes abroad for full-time service under a contract of employment, he will normally be treated as being not resident and not ordinarily resident from the day following his departure until the day before the date of his return. This applies if the following conditions are satisfied:

(1) all the duties of the employment must be performed abroad, or any duties performed in the UK must be only incidental to the overseas duties; and
(2) the absence from the UK in the employment must be for a period which includes a complete tax year; and
(3) interim visits to the UK (leave, etc.) must not amount to more than six months in any one tax year, or three months per year over four years.

For this purpose the overseas employment should be a new employment, separate from the former employment in the UK. This will assist not only in establishing non-resident status but also in obtaining maximum deductions if, in the event, non-residence is not accepted.

12.3.1   Husband and wife

A wife's residence status is independent of that of her husband. If a man is employed full-time abroad, and his wife goes with him but returns before she has been away for a complete tax year, she will remain resident in the UK. If the residence status of the spouses differs in this way, husband and wife are treated as separate individuals for UK tax purposes, unless this is to their disadvantage.

12.3.2   Available accommodation

If a person goes abroad *other than* for full-time employment, and has accommodation available for his use in the UK (whether he owns it or not), he is treated as resident in the UK for any tax year in which he sets foot in the UK at all. This rule *does not apply* to someone with a full-time overseas employment, only performing incidental duties in the UK. (See also 13.1.)

12.3.3 Procedure

When an individual leaves the UK, he is required to complete a questionnaire (from P85) so that the Revenue can give a provisional ruling as to his residence status. Professional advice should be sought in completing this form.

12.4 Employment earnings of non-residents

The basic rule is that non-residents' employment earnings are taxed in the UK only in so far as they are attributable to any duties of the employment which are performed in the UK. In instances where duties are carried out partly in the UK and partly overseas, separate contracts of employment are strongly recommended.

If the duties are normally performed overseas, any duties in the UK will still be treated as if they were performed overseas provided that they are *merely incidental* to the overseas duties.

As to whether UK duties are 'merely incidental' the Inland Revenue take into account the nature of the duties and their relationship to the overseas duties. Common examples are:

(1) *Incidental*

The overseas representative of a UK employer coming to the UK to receive fresh instructions.

(2) *Not incidental*

Company director coming to the UK to attend board meetings; airline pilot landing in the UK, or a courier visiting the UK (among other countries), in the course of his duties (even if not based in the UK).

In general, time spent in the UK is not the deciding factor, but duties in the UK for periods amounting to more than three months in a tax year are regarded as more than incidental. Visits to the UK for training for periods amounting to more than three months in a tax year *are* regarded as incidental so long as no productive work is done in the UK.

In the year of return to the UK, the Revenue authorities do not seek to tax any earnings for the part of the year before arrival. This practice extends to emoluments for any final leave period, even though the leave is spent in the UK.

12.5 Personal allowances for non-residents

Personal allowances for UK income tax are basically only available to UK residents but certain categories of non-residents can claim a proportion of them. The individual must be:

(1) a British subject (including Commonwealth subjects) or citizen of the Irish Republic, *or*

(2) a person who is or has been in the service of the Crown, *or*

(3) a person employed in the service of any missionary society, *or*

(4) a person employed in the service of any territory under Her Majesty's protection, *or*

(5) a resident of the Channel Islands or the Isle of Man, *or*

(6) a former UK resident who is resident abroad for the sake of his health, or the health of a member of his family resident with him, *or*

(7) a widow whose late husband was in Crown service, *or*

(8) a resident and/or national of a country with which the UK has a double tax treaty providing specifically for the relief. The countries are:

Austria	Mauritius
Belgium	Namibia
Burma	Netherlands
Faroe Islands	Netherlands Antilles
Fiji	Norway
Finland	Portugal
France	Singapore
Greece	South Africa
Indonesia	Swaziland
Irish Republic	Sweden
Italy	Switzerland
Kenya	West Germany
Luxembourg	Zambia

(A full list of the countries with which the UK has a double tax treaty is given at 12.6.1)

A British woman married to a national of another country cannot claim as a British subject under (1) above, because claims are dealt with by reference to the husband's status.

The calculation of the relief is in terms of tax, by reference to the actual amounts of UK-taxable income and of world income. The tax that *would* be payable on the world income is worked out as if it were *all* taxable, then the resultant tax is reduced by the fraction:

$$\frac{\text{UK-taxable income}}{\text{world income}}$$

This figure is the *minimum* amount of tax payable, ignoring any double taxation relief (see 12.6).

Example 9
Charles and Daphne are British subjects resident in India, where Charles works, in the tax year 1984/85. They own a house in England, which is let. Daphne receives £3,000 from a trust in the UK. Their UK tax liability would be worked out as follows:

	World income £	UK-taxable income £
Charles's salary	20,000	–
Trust income	3,000	3,000
Rental income (after expenses, UK mortgage interest, etc.)	1,000	1,000
forward	24,000	£4,000

	£
forward	24,000
Personal allowances	3,155
	£20,845

Tax chargeable on £20,845: £6,930

So that the UK tax cannot be reduced below:

$$\frac{4,000}{24,000} \times £6,930 = £1,155$$

The calculation is modified if an individual's income includes UK-source income which bears a reduced rate of UK tax because of a double tax treaty, for example, dividends, interest or royalties. (This does not mean income which is *exempt* from UK tax under a treaty, or income in respect of which tax credit is available – there has to be a limit on the rate of UK tax which can be charged.) The calculation is modified as follows:

(1) *Omit* the income eligible for double tax relief in calculating the income tax payable.
(2) *Omit* the income eligible for double tax relief from income subject to UK tax
(3) *Include* the income eligible for double tax relief in total overseas income and in calculating the hypothetical tax on that income without regard to double tax relief.

Finally, the tax payable by the individual cannot, in any case, be higher than it would have been if the double tax relief had not been available.

Example 10

Edward and Peggy are British subjects resident in France, where Edward works, in the tax year 1984/85. Edward receives £1,000 per year interest income from the UK, and Peggy £3,000 from a UK trust. Under the UK/France double tax treaty, UK tax on the interest is limited to 10 per cent (provided that it is taxable in France). The UK tax would be worked out as follows:

	World income £	UK-taxable income £
Edward's salary	20,000	–
Trust income	3,000	3,000
Interest	1,000	–
	£24,000	£3,000
Personal allowance	3,155	
	£20,845	

Tax chargeable on £20,845: £6,930

So that the UK tax cannot be reduced below:

$$\frac{3,000}{24,000} \times £6,930 = £866$$

(If double tax relief on the interest received had not been available, the UK tax would have been £1,155 as in the previous example.)

12.6   Double taxation relief

If any income of a UK resident – not only employment income – is taxed both in the UK and in an overseas country, relief may be claimed, in whole or in part, from the UK tax either under the double tax treaty or under UK tax rules which provide relief in cases where it is not provided for in an agreement ('unilateral relief'). The details are complex and beyond the scope of this book.

If overseas tax is paid by a UK resident individual, professional advice should be obtained.

When emoluments in respect of which overseas tax has been paid are also taxable in the UK, credit will be given for overseas tax against the UK tax arising from that source. If the overseas tax exceeds the UK tax on those earnings, the tax credit is normally restricted to the UK tax. Where the 100 per cent deduction applies (12.8) no credit can be claimed because the UK tax liability from that source will be nil, and there is therefore no doubly taxed income.

In the case of non-residents, most double tax treaties with other countries provide exemption from UK tax on earnings from employment performed in the UK by a person who is resident in the other country for the purposes of the treaty, under certain conditions. The three basic conditions are usually:

(1) that the employer is, or that the services are performed on behalf of, a resident of the other country, *and*
(2) that the person is not present in the UK for more that 183 days in the tax year, *and*

(3) that the earnings are not borne as such by any UK permanent establishment of the employer.

12.6.1 *The UK's double tax treaties*

The UK has negotiated double tax treaties with most of the developed or developing countries in the world. While some of these are limited to dealing with the double taxation of shipping or air transport profits, the greater number are comprehensive, dealing with the double taxation of all categories of income. These treaties have four main purposes:

(1) to set out comprehensive rules in double taxation situations;
(2) to ensure equal and equitable treatment of taxpayers;
(3) to minimise the number of double tax situations;
(4) to allow tax authorities to resolve conflicts and exchange information.

In any situation involving the possible taxation of income in more than one country, reference should always be made to the relevant treaty.

At present the UK has double tax treaties with the following countries:

Algeria[a]	Belgium
Antigua	Belize
Argentina[b]	Botswana
Australia	Brazil[b]
Austria	Brunei
Bangladesh	Burma
Barbados	Cameroon[a,e]

Canada

China[c]

Cyprus

Denmark

Dominica

Egypt

Ethiopia[a]

Falkland Islands[e]

Faroe Islands

Fiji

Finland

France

Gambia

Ghana

Greece

Grenada

Guernsey

Hungary[c]

Iceland[d]

India

Indonesia

Iran[a]

Irish Republic

Isle of Man

Israel

Italy

Jamaica

Japan

Jersey

Jordan[b]

Kenya

Kiribati and Tuvalu

Korea

Lebanon[b]

Lesotho

Luxembourg

Malawi

Malaysia

Malta

Mauritius

Montserrat

Morocco[e]

Namibia

Netherlands

Netherlands Antilles

New Zealand[e]

Norway

Pakistan

Philippines

Poland

Portugal

Romania

St Christopher & Nevis (St Kitts)

St Lucia

St Vincent

Seychelles

Sierra Leone

Singapore

Solomon Islands

South Africa

Soviet Union[c]

Spain

Sri Lanka	United States of America
Sudan	Venezuela[b,e]
Swaziland	West Germany
Sweden[e]	Yugoslavia
Switzerland	Zaire[b]
Thailand	Zambia
Trinidad & Tobago	Zimbabwe
Uganda	

Notes

[a]Air transport profits only.

[b]Shipping and air transport profits only.

[c]Air transport profits and air transport employees' income only.

[d]Shipping profits only.　[e]Agreement signed but not yet in force.

12.7　Employment earnings of residents

A UK resident is chargeable to UK tax in respect of all emoluments arising from duties performed in the UK. Relief is provided in respect of emoluments arising from all duties performed outside the UK and the form of relief depends on whether the individual is ordinarily resident in the UK or not:

(1) If ordinarily resident

for long absences abroad (over 365 days), a deduction of 100 per cent from the relevant emoluments irrespective of whether they are remitted to the UK (referred to as the '100 per cent deduction', see 12.8);

for short absences abroad (between 30 days and 364 days), a deduction of 25 per cent from the relevant emoluments has been available, but it is proposed to phase this out over the next year (referred to as the '25 per cent deduction', see 12.9).

(2) If not ordinarily resident
remittance of earnings in respect of overseas duties.

(Where the individual performs duties under a single contract of employment partly in the UK and partly overseas, special consideration may need to be given as to the application of the remittance basis to the 'overseas' element of his earnings.)

Where there are separate contracts of employment the allocation of remuneration between these different contracts will need to be commercially justifiable if the two (or more) employments are *associated* with each other. Two employments are *'associated'* if they are both with the same person, or if they are with persons who are associated with each other. A company is 'associated' with another company if one controls the other or if both are controlled by the same person or persons, control being widely defined. An individual or partnership is 'associated' with another person – including a company – if one controls the other, or if both are controlled by the same person or persons. However, an individual cannot be deemed to be controlled by another person.

Subject to this, emoluments qualifying for the 25 per cent deduction (or the 100 per cent deduction) are all relevant earnings (see 2.1) less the following expenses:

133

(1) capital allowances on plant and machinery used for the purposes of the employment;
(2) expenses incurred wholly, exclusively and necessarily in the performance of the duties (see 4.2 *et seq*);
(3) fees and subscriptions paid to professional bodies approved for this purpose by the Inland Revenue (see 4.9);
(4) annual contributions paid under approved and statutory pension schemes.

With regard to pension schemes (see Chapter 10), if the person concerned remains on the payroll of his UK employer – albeit with a separate employment overseas – the deductibility of the pension contributions will not as a rule be affected as long as the contributions continue to be founded on the base UK salary, and not on the base salary plus any cost of living allowances, etc; the continuation of contributions in the event of the overseas employment should be provided for in the pension trust deed. Normally, the rules of an approved pension fund should permit membership to be maintained during temporary secondment abroad.

The 100 or 25 per cent deduction under these rules (see 12.8 and 12.9) is given in *charging* the emoluments to tax. This means that the tax liability is not affected by how much is *remitted* to the UK.

12.8 The '100 per cent' deduction for long absences abroad

The 100 per cent deduction will be available – that is, the emoluments will be tax free – if, in any year of assessment, the duties are performed wholly or partly outside the UK, and any of them are performed during a *qualifying period* (see below) which falls wholly or partly in the year of assessment and consists of at least 365 days.

A 'qualifying period' comprises consecutive days of absence from the UK. Short intervening periods spent in the UK will be ignored provided:

(1) any one period in the UK is less than sixty-three days, *and*
(2) the total of all periods in the UK does not exceed one-sixth of the whole period up to the next UK visit.

A 'day of absence' from the UK is construed strictly and requires that the individual concerned must be absent from the UK at the end of the day in question.

Example 11
Ramsbottom, an overseas sales executive, has spent extended periods abroad in his job, as follows:

Date of departure from UK	Date of return to UK	No. of days absent from UK	No. of days present in UK	Cumulative Totals
1.02.84	1.07.84	151		
			31[a] } 243[b]	
1.08.84	1.10.84	61		
			31[a]	} 425[cd]
1.11.84	1.04.85	151		

^aEach of these periods is less than 63 days, so that test (1) is satisfied.
^bAs the period spent in the UK (31 days) is less than one-sixth of this cumulative total, test (2) is satisfied, except that the cumulative total does not yet amount to at least 365.
^cAs the cumulative period spent in the UK (62 days) is less than one-sixth of this cumulative total, test (2) is still satisfied.
^dThere is therefore a qualifying period of 425 days and Ramsbottom is entitled to 100 per cent deduction in respect of his emoluments for these duties.

Careful planning of return visits to the UK may be helpful in obtaining the maximum benefit of these reliefs.

There is an anti-avoidance rule to prevent 'over-loading' of emoluments for overseas work. The amount eligible for the 100 per cent deduction cannot exceed the proportion of the total emoluments (including those from any 'associated' employments (see 12.7)), as is reasonable having regard to the nature of, and time devoted to, the duties performed outside the UK and to all other relevant circumstances.

The 100 per cent deduction is available even where the overseas employment is changed, provided of course that the new job satisfies all the other conditions.

The effect of periods of leave on the 'qualifying period' depends on whether the leave is spent within or outside the UK.

(1) *Leave spent outside the UK*
    Whether or not this is terminal leave, all days count as part of the 'qualifying period'.
(2) *Leave spent inside the UK*
    If the leave is on termination of the employment, the emoluments will qualify for the 100 per cent deduc-

tion but the leave period will not be part of the 'qualifying period'.

For any other leave, the two tests mentioned above will have to be met to qualify for the 100 per cent deduction

Emoluments attributed to an overseas employment can include emoluments for a *final* leave period after a qualifying period, but not so as to make emoluments for one tax year emoluments of another. (Thus in the above example if Ramsbottom had a final leave period till 31 May 1985 the emoluments for that period would still qualify for the 100 per cent deduction, but they would be assessed, and have the deduction set against them, in 1985/86.)

12.9   The '25 per cent' deduction for short absences abroad

This deduction from emoluments is available if, in any year of assessment, the duties of an employment are performed wholly or partly outside the UK and any of them are performed on a 'qualifying day' which is one of at least thirty such days falling in the year, including qualifying days in *other* employments.

The amount of this deduction for tax years up to and including 1983/84 is 25 per cent of the overseas emoluments. For 1984/85 it is reduced to 12.5 per cent and for 1985/86 and subsequent years withdrawn altogether. For simplicity in what follows, we will continue to refer to the relief under its familiar style of the '25 per cent deduction'.

A 'qualifying day' for this purpose is any *day of absence* from the UK (see 12.8) which:

(1) is devoted substantially to the performance of the duties of that overseas employment or of that and other employments, *or*

(2) is one of at least *seven* consecutive days on which the employee is absent from the UK for the purposes of performing those overseas duties and which are substantially devoted to the job (this covers, for example, a week in Paris including a week-end), *or*

(3) is one on which he is travelling to or from the UK for the purpose of the overseas employment.

The 25 per cent deduction is also available, however short the total period of absence, if in any tax year the duties of an employment are performed wholly outside the UK *and* the employment is with a non-resident employer. If therefore there is any likelihood of the 'thirty-day' requirement being difficult to meet, this arrangement may be worth considering as an alternative to an employment with a UK resident.

To prevent 'over-loading' of emoluments for overseas work, the amount eligible for the 25 per cent deduction cannot exceed:

(1) the 'prescribed proportion' (see below) of the emoluments for the year of assessment, both from the relevant employment and from any associated employments (as defined above), *or*

(2) such *larger* proportion as is reasonable having regard to the nature of, and time devoted to, the duties performed overseas and to all other relevant circumstances. Normally, the Revenue will only allow this

where there are earnings (e.g. commissions) specifically attributable to the overseas duties or where there is a clearly laid-down rate of pay (probably as an established scale) for these duties.

The 'prescribed proportion' is the fraction x/y of the emoluments for the year of assessment concerned, where x is the number of 'qualifying days' in that year, and y is 365 days less the number of days on which the person holds neither the relevant employment nor any associated employment.

Example 12
Broadbottom is employed by Slavedrivers Ltd on whose business he is absent from the UK for sixty qualifying days in 1984/85. He is also employed by Grindemdown Ltd (an associated company) for fifty days in that year in the UK. After a further seventy days working in the UK in 1984/85 for Slavedrivers, he takes an employment with an unconnected employer. The 'prescribed proportion' of his emoluments from the employments with Slavedrivers and Grindemdown for 1984/85 is:

$$\frac{60}{60 + 50 + 70} = \frac{1}{3}$$

12.10   Seamen and aircrew

The places where the duties of seamen and aircrew are deemed to be performed are subject to special rules, and further details may be obtained from H. M. Inspector of Taxes, Cardiff 6 District, Pearl Assurance House, Greyfriars Road, Cardiff CF1 3QP. Telephone: 0222 396831.

12.11 Oil-rig workers

If an individual works on an oil or gas platform in UK territorial waters or in a 'designated area' under the Continental Shelf Act 1964 – broadly any part of the UK sectors of the North Sea, Celtic Sea, etc. – his duties are treated as being performed in the UK. This position may be modified by some double tax treaties, and professional advice should be sought on the point.

12.12 Travelling expenses

The general principles relating to the allowability of travelling expenses for an individual have already been considered in 4.8. As regards such expenses incurred in connection with the overseas duties of an employment, their deductibility depends on two factors:

(1) whether the expenses arise in the course of duties performed wholly abroad ('overseas employment') or partly in the UK and partly abroad ('UK employment'), and

(2) whether the expenses are paid by the employer or are met by the employee from his gross earnings. For this

purpose, expenses paid by an employee and subsequently reimbursed by the employer are treated as having been paid by the employer.

Travelling expenses are always allowable as deductions from the emoluments of the employment if they are for the purpose of taking up an employment or returning at the end of it. Therefore, where such expenses are reimbursed by the employer, effectively the reimbursement is not taxable on the employee. Also, if such a person has *two or more employments*, the duties of one or more of which are performed wholly or partly overseas, the expenses of travelling from the location of one employment to that of another are deductible if *either or both* locations are outside the UK irrespective of the conditions mentioned above. (This covers the case of a man who has jobs with several associated companies in different countries.) In either case the expenses have to be apportioned if they are incurred partly for other purposes.

A deduction is allowed for *board and lodging* expenses outside the UK provided they are incurred to enable the employee to carry out his duties. In the case of an overseas employment the deduction is only allowed if the expenses are borne by the employer, either directly or by reimbursing the employee if he has paid them. *No* deduction is allowed if the employee bears such expenses himself – this is presumably to guard against excessive claims for expenses, the theory being that if the employer bears the cost, he will not allow the expenses to become excessive.

A deduction is allowed, if an individual is absent from the UK for any continuous period of sixty days for the purposes of performing the duties of any employment, for the *travelling expenses of his wife and children* incurred in accompanying him to or from the UK at the beginning or end of the period of absence. A deduction is also allowed for the expenses of a return journey by his wife or by any of his children to visit him during a period of absence or by the individual himself at the end of a period of absence to visit his family, but the number of such journeys by any one individual in a tax year is limited to two. 'Children' include stepchildren, adopted and illegitimate children but not children aged 18 or over at the beginning of the outward journey. These expenses will be deductible irrespective of whether the employment is 'overseas' or 'UK' (as defined above) but they *must* be paid by the employer.

These rules are at present under consideration by the Inland Revenue with a view to some possible relaxation.

12.13   Unremittable overseas income

If an individual cannot remit any overseas income to the UK because of the operation of the law in the overseas country concerned or because of the executive action of its government or because the necessary foreign exchange is unobtainable, he can claim to postpone any UK tax liability on the income until it can be remitted here or brought out in any other way, for example, by conversion into some other remittable foreign currency. Note that liability arises by reference to when the income *can* be transferred and not when it actually is.

12.14   Collection of tax

Where the employer is operating in the UK, PAYE is applied in the usual way (see 3.2).

Where it is clear that the 100 per cent deduction is applicable, a 'no tax' code is issued so that the employer may pay the relevant remuneration without deducting UK tax.

Where the '25 per cent' deduction is applicable, or where it becomes applicable in the course of a tax year as the result of the employee building up more than thirty qualifying days in that year, an allowance may be made in the employee's code for an estimate of the deduction, any adjustment being made on assessment after the end of the tax year.

If the emoluments are paid overseas by an overseas employer, PAYE cannot be applied, and tax will have to be charged by direct assessment on the employee under what is known as the direct collection ('DC') procedure. A provisional assessment is made early in the tax year on the individual, computing his liability to UK income tax on an estimate of his taxable income in that year and this provisional liability is collected from the taxpayer normally in four instalments. At the end of the year when the exact amount of taxable income is known, the assessment is adjusted accordingly. If this gives rise to further tax, this is then collected from the taxpayer; if he is found to have paid too much tax, the excess is either refunded to him or set against his liability for the following year.

12.15 National insurance contributions

If an individual working overseas remains on the payroll of his UK employer, national insurance contributions at the Class 1 rate continue to be payable. After the first twelve months the individual may opt to pay contributions at the Class 3 rate. If the individual is employed by an overseas employer who does not have a place of business in the UK, Class 1 contributions cannot be paid but he can elect at the start of his overseas tour to pay Class 3 contributions to preserve his retirement pension benefits.

Many countries (including all EEC member states) have reciprocal arrangements with the UK and advice should be obtained from any office of the Department of Health and Social Security before proceeding overseas to work for an overseas employer or for more than a year for a UK employer, so as to ensure that the correct amount of contributions are paid.

12.16 Non-tax considerations

It must always be remembered that other countries have different laws and customs from those of the UK and an understanding of these is clearly important to anyone going overseas.

It is particularly recommended that advice be sought on the following matters before entering a foreign country:

(1) level of remuneration required to secure an adequate standard of living;

(2) visas and work permits;
(3) local exchange control regulations (these still apply in many overseas countries and the rules are often strict);
(4) banking arrangements (where residence is retained in the UK no special banking arrangements are usually required other than those required for the provision of funds needed for local living expenses);
(5) health regulations including inoculations;
(6) availability of housing and likely costs;
(7) import duties on household effects;
(8) availability of language courses;
(9) children's education;
(10) possible military service requirements;
(11) social customs and prohibitions;
(12) medical and dental costs;
(13) quarantine regulations for pets, both entering the country and returning to the UK;
(14) driving licences.

Table 12.1 UK Tax Liability on Employment Earnings – Employer Resident in the UK, Employee Domiciled in the UK

Duties performed

Employee's residence status	Wholly in UK	Partly abroad			Wholly abroad		
		Partly in UK	Absent 30 days to 364 days[a]	Absent 365 days (continuous period) not incidental to UK duties	Less than 30 days[a]	30 to 364 days[a]	365 days or more (continuous period)
	1	2	3	4	5	6	7
Resident and ordinarily resident	All	All–subject to columns 3 and 4	1983/84: 75% 1984/85: 87½% 1985/86: All of that part	None	All[b]	1983/84:75% 1984/85: 87½% 1985/86: All	None
Resident but NOT ordinarily resident	All	That part	Remittances from overseas part	Remittances from overseas part	Remittances	Remittances	Remittances
NOT resident	All	That part	None	None	None	None	None

[a]In columns 3, 5 and 6 the number of days of absence must be in the relevant tax year (that is, from 6 April to the subsequent 5 April).
[b]As explained in 12.9, these emoluments may qualify for the 25 per cent deduction if there is a separate contract of employment with a non-resident employer.

13 Foreign Nationals Working in the UK

13.1 General rules

As explained in Chapter 12 an individual may be chargeable to UK tax according to the following basic rules:

(1) If he is resident in the UK, he may be liable to income
tax on income wherever it arises, in the UK or elsewhere. Similarly, he may be liable to capital gains tax
on any disposals of assets, whether made in the UK or
elsewhere. If, however, he is not domiciled in the UK
these rules are substantially modified as regards
income and capital gains arising outside the UK.
(2) If the individual is resident outside the UK, he is normally liable to UK income tax only on income arising in
the UK; further, such liability may be reduced by
the operation of a double tax treaty between the UK
and the country where the individual is resident. Such
an individual may also not be liable to UK capital
gains tax.

Before these matters can be considered in detail for
any particular individual, it is necessary to determine

his tax status in the UK and in particular to establish his 'domicile' and whether he is 'resident' or 'ordinarily resident' in the UK. These terms were looked at in 12.2 and 12.3, but there are certain additional points which should be noted here.

In instances where residence cannot be determined by the rules in 12.3 above, the decision is likely to rest on whether any accommodation is *in fact* available for his use. Any 'available accommodation' for one spouse will normally be treated as 'available accommodation' for the other spouse as well.

Purchase of a house The individual will be regarded as resident from the date of arrival.

Rented accommodation This generally constitutes 'available accommodation' if the period of tenancy is two years or more for furnished accommodation or one year or more for unfurnished accommodation. Where the original furnished tenancy is for a period shorter than two years (or one year for an unfurnished tenancy), it will not constitute 'available accommodation' until this initial period of two years or one year as the case may be has elapsed.

Hotel accommodation This is not normally regarded as 'available accommodation' so that the general rules set out in 12.3 would apply; for example, spending more than 183 days in the UK in a particular tax year would make the individual resident in that year.

Where an individual stays in the UK for an extended period although he does not establish a permanent residence in this country, for example, by buying a house to live in, he would, in the absence of other factors, normally be regarded as ordinarily resident from the beginning of the tax year (i.e. 6 April) in which the third anniversary of his arrival falls.

As soon as the UK Inland Revenue have been informed of an individual's arrival in the UK, they require him to complete certain questionnaires so that they can agree, at least provisionally, his domicile and residence status. Because of the tax consequences which can flow from this, it is advisable to seek professional advice about the completion of these forms.

13.2 Income from UK resident employer

This income is chargeable to UK income tax in full. In particular, a foreign national who comes to the UK to work for a UK company is liable to full tax on his salary from that employment, irrespective of whether it is paid to him within or outside the UK. Similar rules apply to any unearned income arising in the UK such as interest on a deposit account with a UK bank, dividends from shares of UK companies, rents and so on.

13.3 Income from employer not resident in the UK

This income is chargeable to UK income tax by reference to the amount of such income which arises after the individual has become resident in the UK.

Up to the Budget announcement on 13 March 1984, an individual who was paid by an employer not resident in the UK, for example his overseas employer (and this could include the foreign parent company of the UK establishment where he is actually working), could claim a special deduction for UK tax purposes against these so-called 'foreign emoluments'.

Until 13 March 1984, this 'foreign earnings deduction' usually amounted to 50 per cent of the foreign emoluments; thus the individual only paid UK income tax on 50 per cent of his foreign emoluments, so that currently his top rate of tax in the UK could not exceed 30 per cent. However, if in any tax year the individual was resident in the UK in that year and had been resident in the UK in any nine of the preceding ten years, the foreign earnings deduction was reduced to 25 per cent, so that the individual became liable to UK income tax on 75 per cent of his foreign emoluments.

For these purposes, 'earnings' include not only base salary but also the further allowances which are commonly paid to individuals in overseas postings, for example cost of living allowance, foreign service premium, foreign housing allowance, educational expenses. It may also be possible to agree a deduction, before the 50 per cent (or 25 per cent) factor is applied, for expenses analogous to those for which a deduction would have been allowed in the UK ('corresponding payments'). This could cover deductions such as contributions to the overseas employer's pension fund, alimony, mortgage interest on a property in the individual's home country and so on. Except for pension scheme contributions, such corresponding payments were treated as coming first out of the individual's other overseas income which was not chargeable to UK tax, and only any balance could be applied against his 'foreign emoluments'.

Following the announcement in the Budget statement on 13 March 1984, the foreign earnings deduction is being phased out. As regards a non-domiciled individual who was not working for a non-resident employer before 13 March 1984, no deduction will be available at all and the individual will be liable to full UK tax on his emoluments for duties performed in the UK. However, where an individual had already accepted a commitment to take up a UK posting on or before 13 March 1984 and does in fact do so on or before 31 July 1984, he will continue to be entitled to a transitional deduction as set out below.

For a non-domiciled individual who was already in employment in the UK with a non-resident employer on 13 March 1984 and therefore already entitled to the foreign earnings deduction on that day, the relief is being reduced as follows:

(1) for 1984/85 and later years, if the individual was resident in the UK and had been so resident in any nine of the preceding ten years, he will not be able to claim the reduced deduction of 25 per cent mentioned above;

(2) for others, the 50 per cent deduction will continue to be available in the tax years 1984/85, 1985/86 and 1986/87, will be reduced to 25 per cent for 1987/88 and 1988/89 and will be withdrawn altogether for 1989/90 and thereafter.

Example 13
Archie is domiciled in the US and works for the London branch of a non-resident company. He has been resident in the UK since 1966/67. Under the previous rules he was entitled to the 25 per cent deduction from his foreign earnings in 1983/84. Now for 1984/85 and later years, he will not be entitled to any deduction.

Example 14
Bruce is domiciled in Australia and works in London for a non-resident employer. He came to London to work in May 1976, so that at 6 April 1984 he had been resident in the UK for eight out of the ten preceding years. Bruce will qualify for the 50 per cent deduction in 1984/85 but for no deduction at all in later tax years.

Example 15
Carmen is domiciled in Spain and came to work in London for a non-resident employer in June 1983.

Under the new provisions, Carmen will qualify for the foreign earnings deduction as follows:

1983/84	50%
1984/85	50%
1985/86	50%
1986/87	50%
1987/88	25%
1988/89	25%
1989/90	Nil

It should be noted that these rules do *not* apply to individuals who are employed by an employer resident in the Republic of Ireland for tax purposes. The earnings of such individuals are specifically excluded from the definition of 'foreign emoluments', so as at no time to qualify for the 50 per cent (or 25 per cent) deduction.

13.4 Remittance basis

Where an individual, who is not domiciled in the UK but is resident and ordinarily resident here, performs duties for an overseas employer *wholly outside* the UK, the remittance basis applies to the earnings from that employment. This would apply, for example, to an individual who performed certain duties in the UK but who also performed other duties in a parallel employment abroad, for example in European countries. To take advantage of these provisions the duties to be performed within the UK and outside the UK should be clearly distinguished and separate memoranda of understanding defining these should, if possible, be entered into. Care should be taken of the following two aspects:

(1) No part of the duties of the overseas employment should be performed in the UK, except any which are only incidental to the performance of the main duties outside the UK. The term 'incidental' is construed very narrowly in UK tax law and is generally regarded as limited to coming to the UK to report to, or take instructions from, a superior officer or local board of directors in this country. (See also 12.4.)

153

(2) The emoluments attributed to the overseas employment should be settled at a level appropriate to the duties of that employment only, without regard to the duties of the UK employment. There is anti-avoidance legislation aimed at preventing abuse by 'loading' the pay for the overseas employment as against that for the UK employment.

It is strongly recommended that advice be sought before taking up any employment involving mixed duties in this way, as it may be possible to mitigate the burden of taxation in certain circumstances.

Generally, the 'United Kingdom' for this purpose comprises England, Wales, Scotland and Northern Ireland and the territorial waters, at present only up to the three-mile limit, round those territories: it does not include the Channel Islands, the Isle of Man or the Republic of Ireland. However, the area of the UK is extended to include the continental shelf of the North Sea and other waters adjacent to the British Isles, specifically as regards activities in connection with the exploration and exploitation of that area for oil and natural gas. It follows therefore that services supplied by an individual in connection with such activities in the continental shelf area are regarded as services performed in the UK and not outside it.

Unearned income, that is, dividends and interest on overseas stocks, bonds, deposits, etc., rents from real property situated overseas, and so on, continue to be taxed on the remittance basis. That is, an individual who is not domiciled but resident in the UK is only liable to UK tax on the amount of unearned income actually brought into the UK in any tax year. If an individual's income from such sources is substantial, advantage may be gained by remitting from identifiable capital sources, for example savings built up prior to arrival in the UK, as such amounts cannot be taxed as income although there may be some liability to capital gains tax. The way in which suitable banking arrangements may be set up to take best advantage of these provisions is considered in 13.8 below.

13.5   Collection of tax

Where the individual is employed and paid in the UK, income tax (and national insurance) on his earnings is normally collected through the PAYE system, as described in Chapter 3. The Inland Revenue will usually seek to impose this procedure if this is at all possible, for example where an individual is paid by a non-UK office of a non-resident company where that company has a branch office in the UK.

In cases where the Revenue accept that the PAYE procedure is not appropriate for an individual working in the UK who is paid abroad by an overseas employer, the direct collection ('DC') procedure described in 12.14 may be used instead.

13.6   Reimbursed expenses and fringe benefits

Except for some relaxation in the case of certain travelling expenses (see 13.6.1), the same rules apply to foreign nationals working in the UK as regards expenses and fringe benefits as described in Chapters 4 to 8.

Where the individual is employed by an overseas employer so that only 50 per cent (or 75 per cent) of his earnings are chargeable to UK tax, the same treatment will apply to any taxable benefit, whether arising in the UK or overseas, so that only 50 or 75 per cent, as the case may be, is actually liable to tax.

Clearly, it is not possible for the Revenue to obtain details of reimbursed expenses, facilities provided, etc., from an overseas employer, in the way that they can from a UK employer; however, they do have the power to require the UK company or office to which the individual is attached to provide the names and addresses of all individuals working in the UK in this way (though not of any payments or benefits provided for them) and they can call on the individuals concerned to provide the requisite information in their own returns of income.

13.6.1 *Travelling expenses*

As mentioned in 4.8, travelling expenses incurred by an individual in travelling from his home to his place of employment in the UK are generally not deductible as a business expense by the employee; to the extent that they are reimbursed by the employer they will be charged to tax on the employee.

By concession this strict rule is relaxed in the following circumstances:

(1) where the employee is reimbursed the cost of travelling to take up an overseas employment and return from it;

(2) where the employee is separated by reason of his employment from his wife and family, and he is reimbursed the costs of:

(a) a trip to his home country to visit his wife and family;

(b) a trip to the UK by his wife and family to visit him;

(c) a return trip for either (a) or (b);

up to a limit of two such trips in each tax year, provided that he is in the UK for a continuous period of at least sixty days.

This concession also applies to individuals domiciled abroad and employed by an employer resident in the Republic of Ireland for tax purposes, although their earnings do not qualify for the 50 per cent (or 25 per cent) deduction as foreign earnings (see 13.3) above. In the circumstances mentioned above, the same relief applies if the position is reversed and it is the wife who has the overseas employment.

It should be noted that the expenses of removal and relocation incurred by an individual on assignment to the UK or on subsequent reassignment, even where reimbursed in the UK, are generally allowed in full by the Inland Revenue (see 2.3.3).

13.7 Rent paid on UK property to non-resident landlord

It has become an increasingly common practice for UK-based individuals going to work overseas to let their homes in the UK to foreign nationals coming to work on a temporary basis in this country. This is particularly convenient where the respective tours of duty are for comparable periods so that the owner can expect to find his house available for his occupation at least within a reasonable time of his return to the UK.

A foreign-based individual renting property in the UK from a non-resident should take particular note that where he pays the rent direct to the non-resident landlord, e.g. into his UK bank account but not through an agent, he is required to withhold income tax at the basic rate of (currently) 30 per cent from the rent payments and account for this tax to the UK Inland Revenue authorities. The Inland Revenue will make the appropriate arrangements to assess and collect the tax withheld on being advised of the position.

Where the rent is collected by a UK-based agent on the landlord's behalf, he becomes liable to deal with the tax position and the tenant may therefore pay the rent over to him without any requirement to deduct tax.

13.8   Banking arrangements – general

In the case of an individual with foreign domicile, who is in receipt of substantial unearned income and capital gains assessable in the UK on the remittance basis, it is clearly to his advantage to keep his remittances from these sources as low as possible. To substantiate this he should be able, if required, to identify to the satisfaction of the UK Revenue those remittances that are capital, those that are earned income and those that are unearned income.

If he maintained only one bank account overseas, normally there would be credited to it earned income, dividends, interest, etc., and capital sums, including capital gains; the individual would have considerable difficulty in establishing the nature of remittances made out of such a mixed account. This would almost certainly operate to his disadvantage.

This would follow from the Inland Revenue's view of the treatment of remittances from a mixed bank account which is as follows:

(1) any remittance is treated firstly as a remittance of taxable income up to the full amount of the income, secondly as a remittance of capital gains up to the full amount of the gains and finally as a remittance of capital not liable to any tax;

(2) where an exclusively capital bank account is maintained, any remittance from this will be treated as a remittance of capital gains up to the full amount of the gains;

(3) where an individual maintains two capital bank accounts, an amount equal to the original cost of an asset disposed of being credited to one account and the balance representing capital gain being credited to the other, both accounts will be treated for this purpose as a composite fund and remittances will be treated as in (2) above, irrespective of whether the apportionment of sale proceeds between original cost and gains is made by the individual or by his agents.

To avoid this situation it is recommended that an overseas citizen coming to the UK should set up four bank accounts *in his home country before he leaves* as follows:

(1) *Capital bank account*
Credited to his account would be:

(a) the balance standing on all bank accounts as at the date when the individual leaves his country of origin;
(b) the proceeds of sale of any assets owned at the time of departure whose subsequent disposal does not give rise to a potential chargeable gain, either because the sale was made at a loss or at neither profit nor loss, or because the asset or the transaction is outside the charge to UK capital gains tax.

Any remittances out of this account will not be chargeable to UK income tax or capital gains tax.

(2) *Earned income bank account*
This account would only be brought into use after the individual arrived in the UK and it would then have credited to it his salary from his overseas employers. It will be appreciated that the amounts actually remitted from this account will not affect the UK tax chargeable on income from this source.

Where, however, part of this salary is attributable to duties performed wholly outside the UK and therefore taxable on the remittance basis, the salary payments should be divided and paid into separate bank accounts; remittances should then be made from the 'UK duties' account before the 'overseas duties' account is drawn upon.

The UK Inland Revenue have indicated that where a single bank account is used for both 'UK duties' and 'overseas duties' earnings, they will recognise remittances out of it as emanating primarily from the 'UK duties' fund, provided that the employee makes it clear that this was his intention and subject to the 'UK duties' fund being at all times adequate to cover such remittances. To avoid any problems, it is preferable to use separate bank accounts as explained above.

(3) *Unearned income bank account*

This account would be used to receive dividends, interest, rents from properties, etc., arising from sources outside the UK. Any remittance from this account would be chargeable to UK income tax excluding the investment income surcharge.

(4) *Capital realisation bank account*

This account would contain the proceeds of sale of any assets after the individual's arrival in the UK which could give rise to a potential liability to capital gains tax if remitted. Furthermore it should be remembered that if an asset which has been bought out of income or capital gains accumulated overseas which arose after the individual's arrival in the UK is sold and the proceeds of sale are remitted to the UK, then not only will the element of gain be charged to capital gains tax but also the balance of the remittance representing the cost of purchase of the asset will be treated as a remittance of income or capital gains as the case may be and therefore charged to UK tax. Particular care should thus be taken in dealing with such items.

Where an asset is sold prior to coming to the UK but the proceeds of sale are payable by instalments over a period so that some are payable after becoming resident in the UK, the disposal is deemed to take place prior to residence so that no capital gains tax is payable on such instalments. They may therefore be remitted freely to the UK.

13.8.1   *Banking arrangements – husband and wife*

It is recommended that if the wife has income arising overseas, she should also set up four bank accounts in her own name in the same way as her husband so that remittance from her accounts can be identified separately from her husband's. The bank accounts should not be set up in joint names, though there would be no problem in using a joint account that was funded from these separately designated accounts.

It is accepted by the UK tax authorities that if a foreign domiciled citizen makes a gift to his wife consisting of income by alienating the money outside the UK and such money is remitted by the wife to the UK and used by her personally so that her husband does not benefit from or enjoy any part of the gift, such a remittance is not assessable income. Thus if the individual transferred money from his unearned income bank account to his wife's capital account outside the UK and the wife remitted the money to the UK using it to buy a fur coat or diamond ring, the individual would not be liable to income tax on the remittance. The examples of a fur coat and diamond ring have been taken as they are clearly purchases by the wife which do not benefit the husband. It is recommended that the circumstances of the gift, as to the subject matter, the date and place of making it, should be recorded in writing at the time and retained for subsequent production to the Inland Revenue if necessary.

13.8.2 *Constructive remittances*

Income and gains arising abroad are regarded as remitted to the UK if they are paid, used or enjoyed in, or in any manner or form transmitted or brought into this country. Income and gains applied outside the UK in payment of debts incurred in the UK are also treated as received here. The following examples illustrate what is taxed as a remittance even though no cash enters the UK:

(1) a motor car purchased outside the UK with current income or gains arising outside the UK and shipped here;
(2) goods purchased in a London store with, for example, an American Express card and the account paid through an income or capital realisation bank account outside the UK;
(3) rent for UK accommodation paid to the landlord direct from the foreign country to, say, Switzerland;
(4) a holiday trip booked and paid for in the UK. If the travel agency was asked to raise the invoice from its Paris office and the account settled direct from the foreign bank account to Paris, this would not be regarded as a remittance for tax purposes.

Under certain circumstances, depending on the type of income out of which the constructive remittance has been made, it may not be chargeable to tax until, and unless, the asset concerned is realised in the UK. Thus in example (1) above, if the car had been bought out of current employment earnings or out of capital gains, tax will be chargeable on the amount paid for the car as soon as it is brought into the UK. On the other hand, if it is bought out of unearned income arising abroad, liability does not arise until the car is sold in the UK and then only on the amount of the sale proceeds.

It is in order for overseas unearned income or realised gains to be transferred to Europe, the Channel Islands, the Isle of Man or the Republic of Ireland for holiday spending so long as the funds do not enter the UK either directly or indirectly by way of a constructive remittance.

An individual who has little or no earned income and no investment income and capital gains arising in the UK, but substantial investment income and capital gains arising outside the UK, may live tax free in the UK if remittances made here are not taxable remittances. Special arrangements need to be made and detailed advice should be sought before entering into such arrangements, preferably before arrival in the UK.

Where an individual has no capital resources or savings he may still be able to supplement his living expenses in the UK by means of borrowed money, as the remittance of a loan placed in his capital account will not be taxable. Care must be taken however not to repay such a loan out of income or gains arising overseas while he is still resident in the UK, as such a repayment could constitute a constructive remittance.

In a particular year an individual may find that his UK-taxable income is not sufficient to absorb all his UK tax allowances or deductions. This could happen particularly where the individual is resident for only part of the year, so that his earnings chargeable to UK tax are relatively low but he is still entitled to the full allowances for that tax year. Consideration should be given in these circumstances to remitting further investment income so that these allowances are used in full, thus preserving savings at no cost in tax.

13.9 National insurance contributions

Generally, Class 1 contributions are payable for an employee from overseas from the date employment in the UK begins. However, liability to contributions at the Class 1 rate may be deferred for 52 contribution weeks (counted from the beginning of the contribution week following the one in which he arrives), for a person not ordinarily resident in the UK who has been sent to work here temporarily by an employer outside the UK.

If the employee has come from another member state of the European Economic Community or from a country with which the UK has a reciprocal agreement on social security affecting the liability for payment of contributions, the arrangements outlined above may be modified. Information may be obtained from:

Department of Health and Social Security
Overseas Group
Newcastle upon Tyne
NE98 1YX

13.10   Non-tax considerations

At the risk of stating the obvious any foreign national coming to work in the UK should familiarise himself with those laws and customs of the country which differ from those applying in his own. In particular it is recommended that the following should be considered:

(1) level of remuneration required to secure an adequate standard of living;
(2) work permits (not required for citizens of EEC countries);
(3) import duties on household effects, motor cars, etc.;
(4) quarantine regulations for pets, especially on entering the UK.

14 Tax-Planning Hints

14.1 Introduction

Tax planning is a subject in its own right and to cover it in detail is outside the scope of this book. It is the aim of this section to draw attention to some of the tax-planning opportunities which are available to *everyone* in employment. The application of these points does of course depend on the individual's particular circumstances and professional advice should always be taken.

14.2 Pay the correct amount

(1) Make sure all possible allowances are claimed, e.g.

    (a) personal allowance – single or married;
    (b) dependent relative allowance;
    (c) age allowance.

(2) Make sure all possible reliefs are claimed, e.g.

    (a) expenses incurred wholly, exclusively and neces-

sarily in the performance of the duties of the office or employment;
(b) mortgage interest;
(c) other allowable interest payments.

14.3   Tax the correct amount

(1) Employees who work abroad may be able to claim a deduction from the assessable emoluments for the year (see Chapter 12).
(2) Correspondingly, foreign nationals working in the UK may also be able to claim a deduction from their assessable emoluments for the year (see Chapter 13).
(3) Employees may have little choice as to the amount of emoluments they receive. Directors do have some control over the matter. If the company is making a loss for which relief is not immediately available do *not* draw excessive salary. The loss, upon which tax relief may not be immediately available, is increased and PAYE tax is payable *now* on the emoluments. If the company is making a profit, consider the rates of tax being paid by the company and the directors. Tax can be saved by voting remuneration to the directors at the right level.
(4) Always utilise personal allowances, even when reducing directors' emoluments due to company losses. Losses can be carried forward and used in a later year, personal allowances cannot.

14.4 Lump-sum payments

When receiving a lump-sum payment at termination of employment it is wise to keep other income as low as possible. Consider the following:

(1) If trading, maximise capital allowances and loss claims.
(2) Adjust investments so as to reduce the proportion of high-income-earning investments in the year in question. (Possible capital gains tax implications.)
(3) If appropriate, waive remuneration and dividends. (Possible capital transfer tax implications.)

14.5 Benefit from benefits

(1) An employee earning less than £8500 (as defined, see 5.4) should ensure that benefits are provided in such a way that the primary contractual relationship is not between the employee and a third party. Benefits should not be provided by way of exchangeable vouchers or credit cards.
(2) There are considerable tax planning opportunities in the area of provision of employer-owned assets for directors and higher-paid employees. Care is essential in the implementation of schemes devised for this purpose.
(3) An employee who is offered a company car (see Chapter 7) will have to decide whether it is better to receive a mileage allowance or accept the car. From the em-

ployer's point of view the greater an employee's mileage the stronger the case for giving him a company car.

(4) If an employee does accept a company car, any contribution that he makes towards his employer's cost in making the car available should, as far as possible, be applied towards the employer's running costs, thus reducing the relevant scale benefit, rather than towards the provision of private petrol, where no reduction is applicable (see Chapter 7).

14.6 Beneficial loans

If certain rules are followed, employees earning less than £8500 per annum can take advantage of beneficial loans without any tax liability arising (see Chapter 8).

14.7 Educational assistance schemes

Over the years, many schemes have been devised for providing educational assistance to the children of employees, particularly directors/higher-paid employees, with a view to avoiding tax liabilities on those employees. The tax effect of some of the possible arrangements are outlined below:

(1) Loans to employees earning under £8500 are not taxable (see Chapter 8).

(2) Employers may arrange insurance on behalf of a number of employees. Each employee will be taxable on the part of the premium attributable to him.

(3) It is possible to form an educational 'charitable' trust of a type that is specifically exempt from UK taxes, to which the employer makes covenanted payments. Such a trust may make discretionary payments to specific individuals (taxable) or award scholarships (non-taxable). The latter will of course need to be based on academic merit and be non-discriminatory (e.g. between children of say, higher-paid and lower-paid employees).

As regards scholarship payments made after 15 March 1983 to a child where the parent is a director or higher paid employee, the amount will be taxed on the parent as a benefit (this reverses the decision in the so-called 'ICI scholarship' cases).

There are two exceptions to this charge:

(a) where
   (i) the scholarship was awarded before 15 March 1983, *and*
   (ii) the first payment under the award was made before 6 April 1984, *and*
   (iii) the scholar is receiving full-time instruction at the same establishment as that which he was attending when the first payment under the award was made, except that if there is a change of establishment prior to 6 April 1989 the exemption will normally continue until the scholarship expires or 5 April 1989, whichever is earlier.

(b) in the year in which the payment is made, not more than 25 per cent of the awards (by value) would (were it not for this exclusion) give rise to a charge under these provisions.

(4) It is also possible for employers themselves to fund scholarships at particular schools, taking advantage of the fact that scholarship income is not treated as taxable income of the child.

Here again, a benefit in kind charge will arise to the parent of a scholar as described in (3) above and the same exceptions are available.

Deeds of covenant for a child over 18, who for example is a student and therefore has little or no taxable income of his own, are a useful means of supplementing the child's resources. The initial documentation must be prepared with care but once the arrangement is approved by the Revenue the claims for the refund of tax are straightforward to make.

14.8 Remuneration or dividend?

It was always a generally accepted principle that where there was a choice it was more advantageous to pay remuneration out of a company than to pay a dividend. This applied particularly to the situation of individuals who were both directors and shareholders, typically in the context of the 'family' company. The reasons for this were:

(i) in the company, the payment of remuneration was generally deductible for corporation tax at rates varying between 38 per cent and 52 per cent, depending on the level of the company's profits. On the other hand, a dividend is paid out of a company's after-tax profits and can only give rise to effective tax relief in the company of 30 per cent;

(ii) so far as the individual was concerned, investment income (which includes dividends) attracted a surcharge of 15 per cent on top of the rates of tax applicable to earned income (including of course remuneration).

Thus it was generally possible to pay a significantly higher level of remuneration than of dividend before the marginal tax rate of the recipient individual matched that of the paying company.

However, certain changes announced by the Chancellor of the Exchequer in his Budget on 13 March 1984 have reduced the bias against investment income, as follows:

(a) the rate of tax applicable to companies has been reduced immediately. A lower rate of 30 per cent now applies where the taxable profits (subject to certain conditions) are less than £100,000, while the normal rate (where profits exceed £500,000) is being progressively reduced to 35 per cent;

(b) the 15 per cent surcharge mentioned in (ii) above has been abolished for the tax year 1984/85 and subsequently.

The effect of this is that for tax purposes there may be a relatively small, if any, difference in the tax effect of the payment of remuneration or of a dividend, either for the company or for the individual.

In determining what may be the best choice in any particular situation, the following factors should be considered:

(1) The impact of national insurance contributions. These are payable by both employer and employee up to a certain level of remuneration but do not arise at all in relation to dividends (see Appendix C). On the other hand, failure to pay contributions may reduce the employee's entitlement to future benefit;

(2) The facility to pay contributions into an approved pension scheme (see Chapter 10). Again, this arises in relation to remuneration but not to dividends;

(3) The timing of higher rate tax liabilities on the individual. Where remuneration is paid, any higher rate tax is normally collected through the PAYE system by deduction at source at the time of payment; a dividend is treated as if it had suffered tax at source only at the basic rate of 30 per cent and any liability due at higher rates is assessable on the individual later, with the tax due and payable not earlier than 1 December following the end of the tax year in which the dividend is paid;

(4) The timing of the payment over of tax liabilities by the company. As explained in 3.2, PAYE (and national insurance) have to be accounted for, as they are deducted from employees' pay, on a monthly basis; when a company pays a dividend, it is required to account for the deemed basic rate income tax attaching to that dividend, as if it were an advance payment of corporation tax, on a quarterly basis.

14.9 A final word

It will be seen that the system of taxing income from employment is far from simple but that it does offer opportunities for planning. Although this book will not have covered every situation, it may have drawn the reader's attention to some ideas calling for further consideration. It may if nothing else suggest to the reader some questions which he should ask his professional adviser!

Appendix A

Personal Allowances 1984/85

	£	
Single person's allowance	2,005	
Wife's earned income allowance (maximum)	2,005	
Married man's allowance	3,155	
Dependent relative – male claimant	100	
–'single' female claimant	145	
Daughter's or son's services	55	
Blind person's relief	360	
Additional personal allowance ('single parent' families)	1,150	
Widow's bereavement allowance	1,150	
Single person's age allowance	2,490	Income limit
Married man's age allowance	3,955	£8,100
Life assurance premiums paid on policies in force on 13 March 1984	15% deduction from total premiums paid	

Note: Detailed rules as to the entitlement to any of these allowances will need to be checked in individual cases.

Appendix B

Rates of Income Tax 1984/85

Rate %	Band of taxable income £	Cumulative tax £
30	1–15,400	4,620
40	15,401–18,200	5,740
45	18,201–23,100	7,945
50	23,101–30,600	11,695
55	30,601–38,100	15,820
60	over 38,100	—

Appendix C

National Insurance Contributions 1984/85

	Not contracted out	Contracted out
Employee's contribution– standard rate	9%	9% of earnings at lower earnings limit, plus 6.85% of earnings between lower and upper earnings limit
Employee's contribution– reduced rate	3.85%	3.85%
Employer's contribution*	11.45%	11.45% of earnings at lower earnings limit plus 7.35% of earnings between lower and upper earnings limit
Lower earnings limit	£34 p.w.	£34 p.w.
Upper earnings limit	£250 p.w.	£250 p.w.

*These rates include a 1% surcharge (abolished from 1 October 1984)

Appendix D

Benefits in Kind – Cars and Car Petrol 1984/85

	Cars		
	Under 4 years old £	4 years old or more £	Car petrol £
A Cars with original market value up to £16,000 and having a cylinder capacity:			
1300 cc or less	375	250	375
1301 cc–1800 cc	480	320	480
more than 1800 cc	750	500	750
B Cars with original market value up to £16,000 and not having a cylinder capacity: original market value			
less than £4,950	375	250	375
£4,950 – £6,999	480	320	480
£7,000 – £16,000	750	500	750
C Cars with original market value over £16,000			
£16,001 – £24,000	1,100	740	750
over £24,000	1,725	1,150	750

(*See Notes on p. 180*)

Pay and Perks

Notes

(a) Where there is preponderant business use (defined as more than 18,000 miles a year), both the car and car petrol benefits are reduced by half.

(b) Where the car is not available for a period of time (normally at least 30 consecutive days in a year), both the car and car petrol benefits are reduced proportionately.

(c) Where the car has only insubstantial business use (defined as less than 2500 miles a year) or it is an additional car provided by the employer, the car benefit is increased by a half. There is no increase in the car petrol benefit.

(d) The car petrol benefits only apply to cars made available by the employer; the normal benefit-in-kind legislation applies where petrol is provided by an employer for an individual's own car, hire car, etc.

Appendix E

Income from which Tax Cannot be Deducted at Source

---

(1) Living accommodation provided for an employee and/or spouse.
(2) Gift vouchers, etc., given at Christmas or other holidays or as a bonus.
(3) Gifts in kind, e.g. Christmas hampers.
(4) Luncheon vouchers in excess of 15p per day (see 2.3).
(5) Employee's liabilities borne by the employer (e.g. employee's share of national insurance contributions).

Notes
(a) This list is not fully comprehensive.
(b) The employer is required to make a return of these items at the end of each tax year, even though they are not to be included as pay and shown on the deduction working sheets.

Items Not To Be Included in 'Pay'

---

(1) Payments of, or contributions towards, expenses that were actually incurred by the employee in the performance of his duties (see 4.6).
(2) Rent-free accommodation in which the employee resides because of the nature of his employment, or free board and lodging made available by the employer.
(3) Allowances for extra living expenses incurred by employees working temporarily away from home,

provided that they are no more than reasonable amounts.

(4) Luncheon vouchers not in excess of 15p per day.
(5) Termination payments up to certain limits (see Chapter 11).
(6) Benefits under the Workmen's Compensation Acts.
(7) Allowances under the Job Release Act 1977.

Notes
(a) This list is not fully comprehensive.
(b) The rules are modified for directors and higher-paid employees – see Chapters 5 and 6.